# COMING HOME

To Suzanne, Aaron and Norma

Nov. 4/02

To Joan Snyder
Ron Evans

# COMING HOME

## Saskatchewan Remembered

## Ron Evans

THE DUNDURN GROUP
TORONTO · OXFORD

Publisher: Anthony Hawke
Copy-Editor: Natalie Barrington
Design: Jennifer Scott
Printer: Transcontinental

**National Library of Canada Cataloguing in Publication Data**

Evans, Ron, 1936–
Coming home: Saskatchewan remembered

ISBN 1-55002-379-9

1. Evans, Ron, 1936– 2. Saskatchewan — Anecdotes. 3. Saskatchewan — Biography.
4. Saskatchewan — History. I. Title.

FC3511.8E83 2002     971.24'03'092     C2002-901091-8     F1071.6.E83 2002

1   2   3   4   5       06   05   04   03   02

 Canada

THE CANADA COUNCIL | LE CONSEIL DES ARTS
FOR THE ARTS | DU CANADA
SINCE 1957 | DEPUIS 1957

ONTARIO ARTS COUNCIL
CONSEIL DES ARTS DE L'ONTARIO

We acknowledge the support of the **Canada Council for the Arts** and the **Ontario Arts Council** for our publishing program. We also acknowledge the financial support of the **Government of Canada** through the **Book Publishing Industry Development Program** and **The Association for the Export of Canadian Books**, and the **Government of Ontario** through the **Ontario Book Publishers Tax Credit** program.

Care has been taken to trace the ownership of copyright material used in this book. The author and the publisher welcome any information enabling them to rectify any references or credit in subsequent editions.

*J. Kirk Howard, President*

Printed and bound in Canada.⊛
Printed on recycled paper.
www.dundurn.com

Dundurn Press
8 Market Street
Suite 200
Toronto, Ontario, Canada
M5E 1M6

Dundurn Press
73 Lime Walk
Headington, Oxford,
England
OX3 7AD

Dundurn Press
2250 Military Road
Tonawanda NY
U.S.A. 14150

# COMING HOME

# table of contents

# introduction

I was born in a midwife's house in Saskatchewan in 1936. With the exception of eight years, I have lived here all my life. I worked for four years as a parish minister, and the remainder of the time as a chaplain and teacher in both general and psychiatric hospitals. Values centred on family, religion, and sex were the next thing to sacred. "Getting ahead" was my mantra. Hard work and education assured that progress would prevail.

That world has largely disappeared, dissolved like mist on a prairie morning, a wisp or two left in the low spots.

One thing remains: stories.

Some of the stories that follow originate from my immediate family and the cast of characters that made up the community in which I grew up. Others arise out of my relationships with my wife and children, and from years spent working in hospitals and churches. Death — loss of one kind or another — runs like a thread through much of what I have written.

Not to be overlooked, however, is the effect of location — the land. For some, this can mean the mountains or the seacoast, perhaps the city they grew up in. In my case, it means Saskatchewan, and more particularly a distinctive land formation in the central part of the province, referred to with an ambivalent affection by those of us who lived there as "the hills."

A view of Allan Hills, better known as "the hills," an area of rough, rolling land in central Saskatchewan beginning about twenty miles southeast of Saskatoon and covering 450–500 sq. miles.

You might say I possess a kind of language which I am only now learning to understand. I don't mean the English we speak with an accent that amuses Americans, the "outs" and "abouts", and the "eh" for which we are famous. I'm referring rather to a kind of dialect, stories and memories which arise from a particular group of people and a peculiar piece of ground. Telling such stories becomes a means of maintaining my language and keeping in touch with the land that bore me, a way of remembering who I am. I believe it is an essential task to which each of us is called to attend.

# at my father's table

"What was the story on Betsy? Do you know about that?"

We have finished dinner and are sitting about the table looking through a box of old pictures that belonged to my mother. Most are old black and whites of people we once knew, but have all but forgotten. My sister's question has been prompted by a snapshot of a woman who lived a few miles from our farm.

"She got pregnant." I go on to name the man I think was responsible. It's not so much I know this as fact but more a kind of shadow, a dim awareness that has always been there, probably a leftover from a story I heard my father tell.

"Oh heavens, I didn't know that," she says. "I don't seem to have all these details. Ross and you do, but I don't. Where was I when all this was going on?"

I have been pondering that same question, but have no answer for it. Five years older than myself, I assumed she would be a source of information on our family and the community. Yet, she seems strangely unaware of our history. Those events she does recall tend to remain at a certain level of information, more details than a story. With a little nudge, I can elicit all kinds of tales from my brother, incidents involving this character and the other, scandals, the struggles of the "dirty thirties." But not my sister, a person who lived in the same home, as far as I know had the same parents, and went to the same schools. Why then this apparent amnesia when my brother and I remember?

It's the kind of family issue you don't like to ask about for fear it's like an old sweater: pull one thread and the whole thing unravels. Of course, ever the therapist, I have begun to analyze and diagnose. She can't bear to talk about our family, embarrassed about the whole scene. Or maybe some trauma occurred, too painful to remember. Lost memory syndrome?

Sitting at the table with the pictures, I wonder where the discussion will lead. I am about to focus on another picture and escape the discussion entirely when her husband breaks in with an insight, that is, one of those half-formed thoughts that a mind stumbles over, not quite sure what has been unearthed.

"You know," he says, "girls never sat and heard stories the way boys did. Like you and your brother. The men of the community came to your home ... they came there for all kinds of reasons, sat at the table and talked with your dad — and you were there. Or you went with him. You got to hear all the stories. For some reason the girls ..." His voice trails off as if he is sorting through what he has just said.

At once I know he's right. Our questions have been answered, and not by a therapist. It's as if the binoculars have been adjusted ever so slightly and the picture suddenly becomes clear: Father, our kitchen table, and the stories.

Father built the table himself and covered it with linoleum leftover from when he repaired the floor. An Irish neighbour looked at it and said, "By God, Alex, when you're drunk you won't know if you are eating off the floor or the table." Certainly, there were enough times when Father and his friends could have made that mistake.

Father presided at the head to my left, Mother to the right, my brother across, and my sister at the end. We were expected to be there for breakfast at seven, dinner at twelve, and supper at six. In the intervals between, we worked or went to school. For six days this pattern prevailed; on the seventh, in keeping with the work habits of the Almighty, we "rested." Although the meaning of that word was never clear. The Roman Catholics went to church; Protestants, at least the ones with whom I was familiar, seemed just to take a deep breath and get ready for Monday.

Without realizing it, that table has remained a place of refuge and return, a patch of firm ground in memory.

Winter 1936. The story goes that Mother and Father have been away for the afternoon and arrive home just before supper. By this time it is dark, and as Mother enters the kitchen she senses there is someone there. She lights a coal oil lamp and in the half-light finds the room filled with men. They have come looking for my father, and have settled down to await his return. As reeve of the municipality, they are seeking his help in obtaining "relief", the term used to describe what later became welfare, and still later, social assistance. He can authorize their obtaining food to feed their families. As my father listens to their concerns, Mother rushes about peeling potatoes and finding enough meat to make the visitors supper. My brother remembers such occasions and not being able to sit at the table because every seat was taken. I wasn't there, of course, but I have heard the story so often I sometimes believe I was.

Variations on this scene are repeated over the years. Even when the good times returned, it was common for residents of the municipality to arrive in our yard at any time of the day or night. A man wants a better road built to his farm. Or the municipality has a bit of work available and he wants the job. Invariably the visitor and my father would end up at the kitchen table drinking tea, sometimes something stronger, discussing the issue at hand as well as the gossip of the day. One man showed up with a list of voters on which he had marked the people he thought would vote for him. Father was quite sure the man was mistaken, and pointed to several individuals that could not be counted on for support. Finally, in frustration the man stabbed a finger at the page and said, "Well, there's two names I can count on, myself and my wife." Then he paused, drew a line through his wife's name and muttered, "No, damn it, there's only one."

Saturday morning. A police car proceeds along the road leading to our house. It's the Mountie from Hanley, a town thirty miles away. We know he will come into our yard. Every year in the summer he comes like this;

"showing the flag" as the British would say, his way of assuring everyone a police force exists and that law and order prevails. What better way to spread the word than to stop at the reeve's house. He and Father sit at the table and talk while dinner is prepared. The Mountie reports that homebrew is being sold in the community and the source exists somewhere close at hand. Later at school, I can report that the Mountie had dinner with us, but am told to keep quiet about the homebrew.

A doctor calls with a message that a man has died, the father of a neighbour who lives a mile away. Such calls are not uncommon. We have a telephone, while some neighbours do not, with the result that we become messengers, most often bearing bad news. On this occasion, Father and I travel by team and sleigh to tell of the death. I remember the day very clearly, the sun was shining and a coyote trotted across the trail in front of us. When we arrive at the farm, a man comes out to greet us and invite us in. I expect he knows the reason for our visit. As we find our chairs and exchange the customary comments on the weather, I wonder how Father will tell him what has happened. After a moment he says, "Well, Lloyd, there's some bad news. Your dad died this morning." The man nods and says nothing, but there are tears in his eyes. His wife makes us tea, the men talk a while longer, and then we leave. I am proud of my father, that he could speak so clearly, and gently.

I was there for the stories. But that's only part of it. You never just tell stories. To tell stories you need a kitchen and food. A table. And while it may seem unfair to say, I believe you need a father to teach you what's important. A father who keeps telling the stories until they accomplish the purpose for which they were sent.

# "years ago down east ..."

The moment I heard these words I knew we had entered the mythical land of Quebec-Brownsburg and Lachute, towns where Father had grown up. We had gone back to the beginning.

"... it was the middle of July, hotter than hell. The dray man had hauled a barrel of molasses from the train up to the store. He and old Tom were unloading it ... Something slipped and the barrel hit the gound. Cracked the end open. The dray man leaped and heaved the barrel up on its good end. Saved half the molasses. But Old Tom was so damn mad he gave the barrel a kick, knocked it over, and they lost the whole works. And there was the dray man up to his arse in molasses."

If you had told my father he was a storyteller he would have looked at you in disbelief, unsure of what you meant. Yet, he was a superb spinner of tales. The ordinary joke he couldn't tell, forgetting details and invariably getting the punch line wrong. But the events of his own life came alive with every telling. There were stories about the river the boys swam in, and the huge firecrackers they set in fresh cow pies — the risk always being that they wouldn't run fast enough. There was the distant figure of his father, Big John, who had worked in the mines and had died when my father was only three. Legend had it that in the fall of that year at a town fair a fist fight erupted as some of the men sought to settle a disagreement. Big John died soon after the fight as a result of injuries he received. I had heard some of the tales dozens of times, yet I looked forward to each new telling as if it were the first.

My parents near the beginning and approaching the end.

When the stories began "Years ago..." and we had "come west", I knew it was 1918, when Father, a youth of eighteen, had first arrived in Saskatchewan looking for land and a home for his mother, step-father, and younger brother. He spent the winter in Saskatchewan working with an older man looking after a herd of horses.

"... it was in the winter and we were in that old shack. I'll never forget the first night. We had a fire in the stove and had crawled into bed. All of sudden I woke up to find this old bugger swatting the bedsheets and cursing. The shack was full of bedbugs. The heat had them all up and going. But the funny thing was the damn things didn't bite me." As a child it was one of the stories that added to the mythology, the sense of invincibility, that surrounded my father: bedbugs didn't bite him.

There were other stories that began "Back in the thirties ... " We had moved ahead now to events born in hardship and struggle, but, by the time I heard the stories, they were accompanied by a kind of laughter, an expression of emotion that is part disbelief and part gratitude.

"... it was in the middle of July. The phone rang. Johnny Black had taken a fit and died. He had them all the time and if there was no one there to help him he was in trouble. This time he swallowed his tongue. His sister wanted somebody to come and get him ready because they had no money for an undertaker. I picked up Howard Burbridge and we went up there to see what we could do. What his sister hadn't told us was that Johnny had been dead for two days and they hadn't done anything — left him in his room, if you can imagine, a little bit of a place upstairs in that old house, with the windows closed. It smelled something God awful. But we shaved him and got him dressed. When I took Burbridge home that night, Gladys wouldn't let him in the house until he scrubbed himself out at the well. I'll never forget trying to swallow my tongue all the way home — I couldn't do it."

With the stories came people, a rich cast of characters: Carl, a bachelor who had various girlfriends, but never a wife; Andrew, Andy, or Andy Gump, depending on which name you preferred; Major Lees who had fought in India and had a pith helmet; Albert McNaughton, "old Mac", who went mad; Mrs. Fountain, the nurse; the school teachers who came and went, except for the ones who married and stayed to farm and raise a family. Here and there appeared a preacher or a priest around whom there existed a peculiar ambivalence; they were vital for funerals, weddings, and all occasions of ceremony, but looked upon at other times as inconsequential. And then there were a select few, friends who were closer in some ways than blood relatives.

Sunday afternoon. The wind is blowing. It hasn't rained in a month and the crops are suffering in the heat. I can hear the worry in my mother's voice. The worry is there in my father, too, in his eyes, but he says little. We are at the kitchen table. Mother has cooked a chicken. Then we hear a car drive in; Frank and Barbara, as they often do, have stopped for a visit. When their first child was born, Barbara had needed blood because of complications with the birth. Transfusions being a relatively new development, there was no supply of blood available. Father, with the same blood type, was called on to contribute. It was observed later that the blood was surely of high quality in that Father would have consumed enough alcohol to have ensured its purity.

"Stay for supper," Mother says.

It is the opening of a ritual enacted over and over again, common to the farm: arrive

Barbara and Frank Pavelich. Although younger by several years they were my parents' best friends.

unannounced, apologize and refuse all offers of food, but stay — as you had intended to do in the first place. There are many such rituals which everyone knows by instinct, or is expected to know. If you are stuck in the snow and a neighbour pulls you out, an unwritten law requires that you offer him payment. If you do not, you became a "God damn cheapskate." Another law, equal to the first, dictates that if you were the one who provided the assistance you must refuse all payment. If you accept, you became a "God damn chiseller." You learn this kind of thing; if you can't, you don't last. You become the preacher who went back east or the teacher who moved to Vancouver.

"No, no. We just came for a minute. You weren't planning supper for us."

"There's lots," my father assures them. "The new potatoes are ready. The only damn thing that's growing."

They stay. From my room I can hear them talking and laughing long into the evening.

# significant weather

It comes, usually in November, after Halloween. One year it arrived early, in October. Once it came on Remembrance Day. Whatever the time, I recall this day as vividly as a birthday or Christmas.

"Snowed in the night ... not the end of it either." I can hear my father's voice, together with the whistle of the kettle, rising from the kitchen. As was his custom, he has risen at five, put fresh coal in the furnace, made tea, and sat alone reading the paper, waiting for my mother's arrival. There are mornings when the wind blows from the north, slowing the draft on the chimney. On these occasions smoke will drift through the house accompanied by incantations offered up before the reluctant black monster in the basement.

But the wind is in the west this morning, and I lie, deep in the covers of my bed, waiting for the smell of heat. Not the scratching heat of July that parches your face as dry as withered grass. Or the sticky heat of a thunder storm. But winter heat, a drowsy, dusty warmth, spreading now throughout the house, into the walls and ceiling until the house begins to creak, as if complaining at being disturbed. Floating in the half sleep of voices and smells and sounds, I want to stay here forever.

"Those kids don't have anything for their feet."

Instantly I waken. Mother's voice has an edge to it, and even now, fifty years later, the sound is one I want to hide from, sad that she has to feel that way. There should have been new felt boots and overshoes, but the order from Eaton's has not come.

Later we rush about getting ready for school while Mother digs through a trunk in the basement. The mitts and a sweater from last winter still fit, but the felt boots have holes in the toes.

"Some of the kids will have new boots." I hear the words as they leave my mouth, but it's too late. Only years later, when I have children of my own, will I fully appreciate the pain I inflicted.

"Never mind, these will have to do until the order comes." She ties our scarves, then hurries us out the door into the cold to catch our ride to school.

I arrive home in the afternoon to find my father hitching up the team and wagon.

"I want you to come with me to round up the cows," he says. "Get yourself a bite to eat and then we'll go."

The ear lugs of his fur cap stick out at peculiar angles, strings dangling from the ends. With his mitts and boots he looks like a character out of the comics.

In due time I return, ready for what I know lies in store.

"You stand up front and drive." He hands me the reins and we set off across the field.

Even though I am only ten years old, I know what is happening; he wants to teach me how to drive horses, how to work. He is testing me to see if I can endure and not complain. Above all, not complain. Later, in the evening when I am upstairs in bed, I will hear him say to my mother, "By God it was cold out there and that kid took it without a peep."

For weeks the cows have been foraging in the open, growing fat on grass and bits of grain left from the harvest. We find them huddled in a slough, sheltered by the willows, a forlorn and sad-eyed lot, bits of ice hanging from the fur on their bellies.

"You stay in the wagon and I'll get out behind. Just turn around and head back the way we came." Father waves in the direction of home then climbs down from the wagon into the snow and freezing mud.

I'm glad to do what I am told, proud of myself. It's not that I like driving horses. In fact, I like nothing about them; they smell and have a stubborn mind of their own. But Father has put me in charge and I can do it, even though my hands and feet are getting cold.

My mind wanders and I find myself back in the kitchen where I have shed my mitts and boots, and crowd close to the wood stove. Mother turns out a loaf of fresh bread from the oven, taps the crusted bottom with one knuckle and pronounces it "done."

"Jesus Christ, look out."

Father's roar jars me from my dreaming. The horses, intent on getting home themselves, have turned too sharply and the wagon box begins to tip. I jump for the high side, jerk the reins, turning the horses, bringing the wagon back to an even keel.

"Go on, go on ... just follow the track."

Father waves me forward and I drive on while he walks behind spreading an oat sheaf on the ground. "Co boss, co boss, cooooo boss," he calls over and over. I have tried to call the cows like this myself, but, at best, they have turned, staring at me, as if to ask, "What ails you?" Between Father and the cows lies a bond like that between parent and child. Half grown calves frisk and play in the snow, while the older cows, familiar with the game, press forward, bellowing and pushing to within inches of my father's hand. Wisps of steam begin to rise from their struggling bodies. Father spreads more oat sheaf, and soon a ragged column of wagon, man, and beast winds across the skyline in the fading light of a winter afternoon.

Later in the evening we will sit in the kitchen waiting for the coals to burn down to make popcorn. We will laugh as Father eats an apple, seeds and all, wiggling his ears at the same time.

On these nights it is easy to fall asleep.


For a considerable time I thought my remembering such days had simply to do with the confusion I felt around each of my parents, reactions which only now I find possible to name. There is sadness in knowing you loved a parent and were loved, that you were very close, but too many things interfered. You would give anything for a little more time. There is a sadness, maybe guilt, in knowing you loved and were loved, but too often it was across a distance. As much as you wanted the distance bridged, as much as you assumed you sought reconciliation, it remained, destined to be there. There's something futile, then, in becoming fixat-

ed on deficiencies in a relationship, a sadness in spending a lifetime identifying faults and correcting injustices, perceived or otherwise.

Even with my parents gone and the farm a distant piece of history,
this same day comes: it arrived today, the 25th of November. At least
ten days late. I try to name the feeling, and then realize my mistake;
feelings are such limited things, suitable for arguments and love letters.
Whatever this day has brought, it eludes my naming. An intuition of
something present.


One of the things I noticed living in California was the weather; there
was none or at least, none as I had come to know it. The conditions
were most often what the forecaster refers to in Saskatchewan as "no
significant weather": sun, little wind, no precipitation. Such days
required only that you change from shorts to long pants in December;
drive three hours to the Sierras for your afternoon of winter; change
clothes for a weekend at the beach. California: one long summer where
it became a duty to be happy, where everything lived and nothing died.

In Saskatchewan, even in a year when most days the temperature
rises above freezing, there can be no illusions. A skiff of snow, a bite to
the wind, and conversations that turn to reassurance: "Well, it's not
that bad; another month and the days will start to get a bit longer."

"You can see a difference in the light by New Years, a brighter white."

"Hard to believe but in six months the sun will rise at four."

But today winter came, not on little cat feet, but in boots and
mitts. Significant weather that set memories in motion and let loose a
mood. And though most of us would refuse to admit it, however much
we wait for spring and welcome summer, it's winter we trust, count on,
disoriented until it comes.

# howling at the moon

A friend of mine is convinced a pack of wolves inhabit a piece of land
he owns smack in the middle of Saskatchewan. When you consider that
no wolves have lived in this part of the country for at least a hundred
years one might suspect that the isolation of a long winter has taken a
toll on the man. But knowing the country involved, I'm not prepared to
dismiss the idea out of hand; there may be wolves in those hills.

My friend's theory is that the wolves are part of a sinister plot by
Ducks Unlimited — all funded by American interests, of course. The
wolves have been let loose as a means of controlling fox and other
small game that feed off duck eggs and the young. Somehow more
wolves means more ducks. The CIA may be involved, but I doubt it. If
we were hiding Cubans back there in the hills, I can see the CIA being
interested. But not when it's wolves. I have my own theory.

I think the wolves are home grown. To appreciate this you need to
know more about the land in question.

Those of us who grew up in the area referred to the territory simply
as the hills. On a map of Canada, even of Saskatchewan, the place
doesn't amount to squat: a stony, rolling chunk of land, no more than
twenty-five miles square, coughed up and left behind by the last Ice
Age. You can travel all day in any direction you like from the hills and
still not get anywhere. Two hundred miles to the south lies the Canada-
U.S. border, an invisible line dividing one empty space from another.
Five hundred miles to the west stand the Rockies. To the east, you can

drive for five hundred miles through farm land and small towns and by chance, hit Winnipeg. (If you're lucky you will miss it altogether.) Two hundred miles to the north, the farm land peters out, but Saskatchewan keeps going for another six hundred miles of trees, lakes, and rocks.

The hills were never large enough to develop the kind of mystique that surrounds the Appalachia region of the U.S. Anyway, Newfoundland with its poverty and isolation — not to mention the accent, jokes, and music — came along in 1949 to become "low man on the totem," robbing us of our identity. Nor was there enough time. Civilization — roads and cars, along with tractors that can pull a city block of machinery — came too soon.

But for a little while they were the hills. When the dust blew or the mud made great black snowshoes out of our feet, they sometimes became "the God damn hills," but, even then, there was a note of affection in our words. Folks in town spoke of the hills in a different voice, that "scruffy-lot-that-live-out-there-in-the-stones-and-dust-and-come-to-town-on-Saturday-night" kind of voice. We didn't mind, not much anyway. Or, maybe outsiders didn't think that at all; it was what we thought of ourselves.


There are two activities, as they were practiced in the hills, that will help explain why I believe the wolves are not strays or CIA plants: homebrew and sex. Homebrew and sex, like wolves, require a certain privacy in order to thrive. In the hills, where the roads end up in trails, and if you keep going you'll find a weather beaten house and a barn with a two-holer in the poplars, the homebrew is almost always good. The sex? I can only go by the stories. Hidden away you could do a lot of things, needed to do a lot of things, in order to keep going. Under these conditions the hills produced their own wolves.


Stories about brew abound, most of them having to do with someone getting caught making it, or of someone drinking bad stuff and becoming deathly ill. A farmer named Stan told a story about his milk cow getting into a batch of mash and staggering about the farm yard. No one can be sure if this really happened. Just as most world religions have a flood story, makers of homebrew invariably have a cow in the mash. The fact that cannot be doubted, one that marks every homebrew story, is that someone snitched on Stan and the RCMP raided his farm. They searched everywhere and were about to give up until, in Stan's words, "one nosy son of a bitch decided to unload the hay rack." There, hidden at the bottom, was the still. Stan spent the winter in jail.

The other piece of that story involves Stan's wife. The letter informing the family that Stan must go to jail contained the line "by order in council." When his wife, barely able to read and not familiar with legal jargon, saw this she immediately thought it meant the municipal council, of which my father was the reeve. To her dying day, the woman believed that the municipal council and my father were responsible for putting her husband behind bars.

Tony made an equally good brew and, because he lived mid-way between our farm and town, his home became a stopping place, a kind of inn for weary travellers in the tradition of the Middle Ages. A jug of homebrew with a pot of cabbage rolls and you had a feast. My father told of being present one winter while the distilling operation was in progress, and of drinking fresh homebrew. With the temperature at -30°C, the roads blocked, and the Mounties twenty-five miles away, no one worried. Alas, Tony got caught, more than once, reported to the RCMP by a spiteful neighbour.

Some of the more memorable stories concerned bad brew. On one occasion my father and the hired man, Dick, got into such a batch. Both managed to make it home, but in terrible condition, the hired man being the worse off. Father laid the man out in a manger of the barn and left him there. He said that if a manger was good enough for Jesus, it was good enough for Dick. Dick crawled out two days later and recovered.

The hills then, despite the police raids, was a place that provided a bit of cover for things like homebrew to thrive. Moreover, it was a place where, evolution left to itself could, perhaps, produce a wolf. This becomes evident when you consider the matter of sexual activities.

I once heard a woman from the Appalachia region in the U.S. tell about a funeral for her uncle, a man considered a model citizen in his town. While some of the relatives sat in the living room remembering how wonderful the man had been, young women of the clan sat upstairs telling how the same man had sexually molested each of them. I don't know if that went on in the hills or not. Perhaps it did, but it was not talked about. Fifty years ago we didn't have the language for such a discussion; we didn't even have affairs in the hills. Incest, adultery, promiscuity: such words came later with diaphragms, partners, and consenting adults. All I remember hearing was my father's phrase, "the bull jumped the fence," a metaphor for all occasions where sex was concerned.

I recall one time the vet stopped at our house after treating an animal on a neighbouring farm. He told my father that the woman of the house had offered her services as payment. He didn't accept. My impression was that he had declined more on the basis of what she had to offer than for any moral reasons. Had he accepted, it would have been a case of "the bull jumping the fence."

There were any number of situations where the bull did make it over. North of us there was at least one case of wife swapping. Another situation involved what you might call "job sharing": one man had been identified as the husband and at least two other men worked the "casual shift." There were two other cases, with offspring to prove it, of families with one mother, but clearly more than one father. You might say two bulls cleared the same fence.

I realize that writing in this fashion can sound a bit priggish, echoing a bygone morality. But for those of us who lived there, we were not overly shocked at these happenings, any more than we were by the homebrew. This is just the way it was.

There was a Ukrainian gentleman by the name of Mike who had a dog with blood lines running back years. The animal had the head and eyes of a wolf, the kind a photographer can catch with a camera where the animal looks out at you and no matter where you go in the room you are followed. I think the mother had been a pup from somewhere in the mountains of the Ukraine. A few miles away there was an Englishman named Lees — Major Lees because he was supposed to have served with the British army in India. He had a pith helmet, a great drooping moustache beneath a slightly elevated nose, all topped off by a British accent. "Back in Indjha, why I rememba once we were outnumbered ten to one. But we held. Empah and all that, you know."

The major had a dog — a sleek, long legged thing, some kind of English hunting dog with a pedigree as long as the major's. One spring, Mike's dog strayed down south and got mixed up with the major's bitch. Jumped the fence. The major was highly offended at this mixing of the races, but the offspring were something to behold, one animal in particular: chocolate brown with the eyes and head of a wolf but the body of a hound.

Well, that's my theory of how the wolves come to be in the hills. Wolves could never make it from the Rockies or the north land; too many miles of civilization. Shot guns or snowmobiles would have got them. Ducks Unlimited? No, I think the crossing of Mike's hound and the major's bitch has produced, years later, some kind of genetic mutation resulting in a super dog that comes close to being a wolf. Home grown along with the brew. Somebody jumped the fence. Or got invited in.

# "15"

I can still see it, a stretch of dirt extending west across the hills, rising and falling like a ribbon in the wind. Officially, it was Highway 15, but to those of us who drove it, it was just "15", and when rain had turned the dirt to gumbo, snow lay in drifts three feet deep reducing all travel to a team of horses, it was "God damn 15."

I say 15 ran west, because in my mind as a child the east was unknown country where strange people lived and where we seldom travelled. We drove two miles south from our farm and turned west at Frank Pavelich's, past Roy Jewell's house high up on a hill, George Wickens' the bachelor, Brunoughs' the Belgians, and Hilledge school. Tony's home held special significance. Going or coming, his farm was halfway, a kind of monastery catering to the needs of weary travellers, where, in winter, with the roads blocked and the Mountie safely in his office twenty miles away, homebrew flowed freely and cabbage rolls were served.

In truth it was as if 15 were only twelve miles long, a string that attached us to town, to the railway, the post office, the grocery store. There was even a furniture maker who made coffins, a midwife's house where I was born, and a church for funerals. Of course, there was a beer parlour — the destination and point of departure for most men who travelled the road.

15 Highway as it appears today. Once famous for its mud and snow it has been rebuilt, the hills cut down and the surface paved — although calling it a highway still seems a little generous.

Running east and west across the province, 15 was built sometime in the 1920s, but never completed. In the midst of the Dirty Thirties it became a make-work project where, instead of wasting away in a relief camp or drifting across country on the rails, men found summer employment. For a time the road stopped two miles to the south of our farm. A few years and another government later, the road was extended another six miles. In time it was completed, joining up with a north-south highway further to the east.

By today's standards, the construction methods seem primitive. Much of the equipment — dump wagons, graders, and a creation known as the Fresno — were horse drawn. The Fresno, depending on how you viewed it, could be seen as the predecessor to modern earthmovers or as one step removed from a pail and shovel. It was simply a rectangular steel container, eight feet wide and two feet deep, open at the front, which when pulled forward by four horses, filled with earth. The unique feature was the Johnson bar, a piece of steel five feet long attached to one side of the bucket and serving as a kind of handle. It may have been named after the man who invented it or after the first man it killed.

Operation of the Fresno required a man to force down on the Johnson bar as the contraption and horses moved forward. To dump the load, he simply reefed up, let go of the bar, and got out of the way. At least this is what was intended. If, however, one were careless, or the bucket hooked a stone, the Johnson bar could be transformed into a lethal weapon — five feet of steel peeling aside any man who happened to be in its path. A Fresno remained in working order on our farm for years, and while I was too young to operate it, my brother often did. I can still hear my father's shouted warning: "Be careful of that damn thing."

While 15 has been rebuilt and paved, like an old mansion re-modeled, signs remain of what had once made it a masterpiece. Imagine a series of rolling hills, the highest perhaps twenty feet. For every hill there is a slough or ravine. Cut a path through the hills and build a strip of earth across the sloughs. Now you have a road — albeit a narrow one, no more than twenty-five feet wide in places. Some have said it is what the poet had in mind when he said every valley shall be lifted and every mountain made low. There's one track down the middle and you go slowly when you meet people. It's the narrow spots across the sloughs, grades we called them, and the drop over the edge that catch your eye. Only one man was killed on 15. He went over a grade riding in the back of a truck during a rainstorm.

My father was the timekeeper and paymaster on the construction crew that built a portion of 15, a position which allowed him to arrange for many local men to find work. A neighbour, Andy, was hired on as the blacksmith's helper. No one was quite sure what the blacksmith's helper did, but the job suited Andy's abilities. Above all, he got paid. Some farmers rented out their horses. Others sold hay and oats for feed, and not infrequently overcharged for it.

Father told a story about one man in particular who had earned a name for his attempts to make a dollar from the road company. There was nothing unique in what he had done; several others had engaged in a measure of the same. This man, however, in addition to being dishonest, had been particularly difficult to work with. The chief engineer, one Mr. Potts, developed a keen dislike for him. On the last day of camp, as the crews were about to move on, Mr. Potts met with the man to settle accounts. Potts, one of the few who owned a good car, was sitting in his vehicle, the window down and the motor running.

"Now Sir, are we square? Are you satisfied?"

"Yes, yes ... everything has been paid." Potts reached out and they shook hands. Smiles all around.

"There is just one more thing I want to say, Sir: You are the dirtiest, meanest man I have ever dealt with. Good day!" Potts eased out the clutch and drove away.

During the summer months, the locals associated 15 with drunks and mud; the two inevitably seemed to occur together, there being degrees both to the depth of the mud and the level of drunkenness. A dry, dusty road could be turned to clinging gumbo in a matter of minutes. I have worked on a car fender plugged so tight with mud that the car could not move. If the rain continued until water lay in the ruts, you slid along quite well. Similarly, with the amount of alcohol in the driver. Just as the increase in water made driving easier, more alcohol in the driver, rather than hindering his driving, seemed to improve it. But this was only for half the year.

By Christmas — or before, depending on the severity of the winter — 15 ceased being a highway for motor vehicles and became a snow trail, a narrow track travelled only by horses and sleighs. If the weather was reasonably warm and the snow conditions good, you could make it to town in two hours. A good team made it in less. On a bad day, it could take closer to three. Christmas cards and Bing Crosby have made sleigh rides something romantic: voices singing, sleigh bells ringing. His experience of sleigh rides is not mine.

We have endured the drive home from town, cooped up in the cutter, a contraption pulled by two horses and named after those sleek little boats that cut smoothly through the water in Halifax harbour or off

A "cutter" to which was hitched a team of horses. While such contraptions were reliable, after a two hour ride, you could not say they were comfortable.

Vancouver Island. Our proud ship — eight-by-six feet and just high enough to sit in, with a window in the front through which you can see the horses' arses bobbing up and down in the cold — is neither sleek nor smooth. In places, the trail has blown bare of snow. Steel runners grind against the gravel emitting a high pitched screech. At other points drifts two feet high have formed at right angles across the trail — hummocks we call them, a word which the dictionary defines as ridges in an ice field. Our cutter climbs up one side of a hummock, teeters a moment on the top, and then drops, smashing onto the hardened snow below, jarring bones and teeth.

The cutter is warm — some of the time. A little stove with a pipe through the roof gives off enough heat to provide a modest degree of comfort. But we have been on the trail for almost two hours. We could have left town in mid-afternoon while it was still light and a little warmer, but we didn't; we waited until the beer parlour closed at six. Our wood supply has run out and my feet and hands have begun to chill. My body hurts. Then the horses turn.

I can't see the trail in the dark. But the horses know. We have left 15, and are travelling north toward our farm. Two miles to go. At once the pace quickens. The trail levels out and our lurching gives way to a steady glide, a little ship under full sail. After the trip into town in the morning, and miles of hard driving on the return, the horses still have something left. And they give it.

We are headed for home.

# in the beginning was the dream

The mother knows only that her daughter was born "when the leaves were falling." No record of the birth appears in any government department. But the school register requires such information. The teacher, who happens to be my mother, is advised by the school superintendent to enter a date sometime in September, in a year appropriate to the child's size. Years later when the child, now a woman, applies for a job, it is the school register to which she turns for proof of her age. Such was the influence of the school.

After family, the school and the teacher were the most important influences in our lives, even church and clergy were but a distant third. I understand now why the school held such a position, but I didn't then; you just went to school because, well because everyone goes to school.

To begin with the law required that a child attend school until he or she completed Grade 8 or reached the age of fifteen. In my family, just as you understood there was to be no sex until you were married, so you knew you were not to leave school after Grade 8. Complete Grade 12 at least; preferably go on to university. Even if you "just wanted to farm," you needed more education. It would assure a better job and the attaining of that elusive goal of "getting ahead." It is understandable, then, why there are stories in every community of the length to which some parents were forced to go to ensure their children could attend school.

1910. My mother's parents are new to Saskatchewan having moved here from Ontario with their four daughters, all of them school age. There should be a school but the school board is dominated by individuals who have bought land on speculation, hoping for a quick dollar. The board members have no children, and effectively block the opening of a school, fearing their taxes will be raised. My grandmother and another woman decide their only hope lies in political action.

The two women travelled to Regina by train where they presented their case to the Minister of Education. While sympathetic, he could do nothing; power lay with the local board. Discouraged, but not defeated, they returned home to revise their strategy and plot new tactics.

The school board consisted of three people all dominated by the chairman, a Mr. Crow by name. The women knew they had the support of one board member, and if one more supporter can be elected they can carry the day. According to the values of the time, a man was required for the position, and one was found. The women then set about campaigning, knowing that with the very limited constituency — a few dozen voters at most — a shift of even one vote can mean success or failure. To this end, they persuaded a supporter to remain living on his quarter section until the votes were cast. Their efforts paid off; their candidate was elected, swinging the balance of power in their favour.

In due time, the provincial government ordered the school opened and the books turned over. Any refusal to do so would result in a fine of several dollars a day. Although Mr. Crow protested, the board voted to open the school. The story goes that Mr. Crow appeared at one woman's home, flinging down the books shouting, "I'll see you in hell before I'll support a school."

She replied, "Then, Mr. Crow, you must intend to go there."

Later, the school superintendent christens the board the Petticoat School Board.


The school, of course, brought with it a person — the teacher. The authority of the school and it's presence in the community found expression through the teacher, almost always a woman. Most teachers were looked up to and wielded power equal to a parent

My mother (fifth from right) with her pupils standing
in front of Silver Lake School in 1924.

even though they were often very young. In the case of my mother she was only seventeen years old when she arrived at her first school. She had completed six months of training at "Normal School," the fast-track program to produce teachers for the schools springing up across the prairie. A number of her first students had had little or no opportunity to attend a classroom. There were some who were taller than her, almost as old, and only in Grade 2. So keen, however, were the parents to have their children in school, coupled with a respect for, if not fear of, authority, that discipline was never a problem.

Sitting at her desk, my mother was confronted one afternoon by several of the younger children screaming, "Come quick! Paul has a knife!" Outside she found one of the bigger boys had cornered two others up against the school wall, and was threatening them with a knife. New to the school, he had just arrived from a part of the world where violence taught him the skill of survival. Speaking little English, some of the local boys teased him until he finally reacted.

"Give me the knife, Paul," my mother says. Quietly, he hands over his weapon and the crisis is over. Until the next day. The mother of the boys Paul threatened, a woman originally from Ontario, arrives at school angry with Mother.

"You should have given that boy the strap," she announces.

"If it had been one of your sons I would have," Mother replies. "Paul only did what he has learned."


Outside the classroom the teacher's authority translated into a position of social prominence. People noticed how she dressed and how she acted. To invite the teacher home for dinner was an honour. However, if she spent too much time with one family a certain tension developed. You might think that a scandal, or at least all the ingredients of one, would cause major upheaval. Yet, when a married man in our community began spending unusual amounts of time at the teacherage, the two-room house on the school grounds, there were few repercussions. Speculation ran high, but strangely no one seemed unduly perturbed. At least no one was blacklisted, no one asked to leave.

I can't be sure, but I suspect there was an allowance being made, an understanding agreed to. In the privacy of their own thoughts, people of the community, especially women, had some empathy for both parties even if they might not admit to it. They were familiar with isolation, of the toll it could take. Sometimes you had to make do with what you had. In this case, both teacher and farmer had found pleasure in the other's company.

As for myself, I didn't care what the teacher did after hours; it was the six and a half hours of each day, five days a week, spent under her charge that mattered.

If a teacher had even a modest liking for children and a measure of common sense, school could be a decent place. If she was a troubled person, lacking in patience and understanding, school became one long nightmare that you thought would never end. I had only one who fell in this latter category, an unstable woman who screamed, threw chalk at children, and in general maintained control by terror. Fortunately, there were others, good women to whom I owe a debt of gratitude for having restored pride and dignity in myself.

School, of course, was more than a person; in addition to the teacher there was the place itself — a building, two acres of ground, and a community of people. Your school district located you in the public mind, placed you geographically, added a little something to your identity.

To the north of us lay Horseshoe Lake School, so named for a nearby body of water that was little more than a large slough in the midst of very rough land, real estate not unlike those who lived on it. To the south lay Lothian, referred to as "the den of forty thieves" because of the number of citizens who had had scrapes with the law. We were from Chatham, named for a district in Quebec. For whatever reason, unlike the names of surrounding schools, the name seemed to bestow a bit of class — or at least we thought it did.

Besides education, the school was the centre of social life. For many years, especially in the deepest days of the depression, you gathered at your local school or a neighbouring one for dances on Friday nights with Mid Rogers on the violin and Marie on the accordion. For the grand sum of twenty-five cents you danced the night away. Mid and Marie were paid a dollar each. For the same two bits, the women served egg salad sandwiches at midnight with chocolate cake and coffee. On other occasions, the Wheat Pool would hold card games, where you played Norwegian Whist and the competition was fierce. There were those who cheated, and others you knew you didn't want as a partner, but when the evening was over it didn't matter. Of course, the highlight of the year was the school Christmas concert, an occasion for the community to gather, and for parents to watch their children sing and perform in ways which must have been quite terrible. But as the weekly newspaper reported, the details notwithstanding, "A good time was had by all."

Schools also made a contribution to family life; they served as marriage bureaus of a sort. Indeed many of us owe our very existence to the school.

In the early years, one obstacle facing rural bachelors wanting to marry was accessibility. How were young men who had set up farm to meet young women? One man said he was going to hire a bus to load up half the church choirs in Saskatoon, then drop them off around rural

A prairie school in 2001 abandoned to the pigeons and the weather.

Saskatchewan — a matchmaking bureau on wheels. For a considerable time, the school system filled the role in a more natural fashion.

Mother goes to a dance and meets a young local man. He has come well-dressed, in a white shirt and tie. Later, she will say, "He was the best looking man in the community." In due time, they marry and set up a farm. Three children follow. A similar process repeats itself a few years later when a young woman arrives in a neighbouring school district. After a year, she marries a local bachelor and they settle two miles from our home. At the time, theirs is an unlikely marriage: she is Scottish-Protestant, he is Croat-Roman Catholic. They raise three daughters and over the years become my parents' best friends. A generation later, one of my favourite teachers marries a man in the community, aided by the matchmaking skills of his mother and aunt. Theirs is a more conventional marriage — both Scots, both Protestant. Again, depending on who was reporting, "A good time was had by all."

These are the details — the good times, the community squabbles, the teachers that came and went, some who stayed, the dances and Christmas concerts — fragments of a story that when you put them all together make a dream, one that kept us going. As I said, we rarely talked about it. Maybe because you often can't recognize a dream until later when you look back and see the remains of it. Or maybe we were afraid to talk about it, afraid that our talking would cause the dream to slip away.

Whatever the case, for individuals like my mother, the dream prevailed. Only through school and an education could one hope for redemption, dream of injustice being corrected. Via an education hopes could be fulfilled, success realized. Books and reading, some new clothes. Maybe even a little travel. Education could make possible what you had been denied. If not for yourself, then for your children. School would achieve the goal of "getting ahead."


So the dream continues. Go to school. Go to university. Education will overcome all obstacles, help keep the dream in sight, like a mirage on a morning skyline.

# landscaping

The boulder lay in some bush by the side of the trail. Bluish grey with a flat place to sit on and a back to lean against. I could see it as plain as the day my cousin discovered it on our way home from school. Though the stone clearly belonged to him, I put a claim on it and we argued over ownership until my sister intervened with a reasonable, even if uninteresting solution: take turns. The rock became our stopping place on hot afternoons, the half-way point on the long walk home. Fifty-odd years later, I realize it is one of those childhood events that probably occurred no more than two or three times before the novelty wore off.

Nevertheless, I remembered that stone and wanted it for my backyard. Enlisting my wife in the project, I drove out to the old farm and tracked down the owner. "Take as many as you like", he commented, amused that anyone should want a rock. Encouraged by his blessing, we set out across the field convinced, at least I was, that we would find the stone just as it had been left years before.

Of course, the search proved futile. The fence line was in a different place. Fifty years of bush and grass had obliterated the trail. The fields all looked different.

About to abandon the project, we came upon another stone, not blue but black and grey with a fuzz of moss growing on one side. It had a flat place to sit and a jagged chunk at the back that one could, with a bit of effort, imagine to be the back of a chair. But at over 300 pounds we couldn't lift it. Not to be denied, we rolled it up a slight rise through dense grass to the edge of a field. Here we looped a rope around it, hooked it to the back of the truck, and dragged it for almost half a mile before we came upon the farmer with his tractor and front-end loader.

By the unwritten code of the land, I knew I must offer to pay him. In fact, I wanted to pay him, would have paid twice what he asked. There was a sadness to the man, a look as beaten as his worn boots and jeans. For an instant I was with my father in the same field, in the heat and dust, picking stones. A job with no beginning and no end.

"How much do I owe you?" I asked, even though I knew the answer.

"Nah, that's all right," he replied, a slight smile crossing his face. It was as if he was pleased that he and his tractor had been of service. And that one of his rocks had been chosen. That's the way it is with farmers, unloved one moment, admired the next. For that matter, with stones, too.

On one particular afternoon of rock picking, I remember bending over to grab a reddish chunk of granite about twice the size of my fist. Suddenly, as if by some special effect, it seemed to transform before my eyes into an oval stone, larger at one end than the other, both ends worn smooth and white, a perfect groove worn around its middle. I had found the head of a stone hammer lost ages before by an Indian traveller. For the rest of the day every stone looked different. But again a stone can be like that; sometimes you even forget it's stone.

Like gazing at Michelangelo's Pietà. Or the Vimy memorial in France, sculpted from white marble and engraved with the names of 11,285 Canadian soldiers missing in action, that is, men blown to pieces, buried, or never found. It's a troubling sight, yet one of the most quiet, serene places I know of. I have heard that the Vietnam wall in Washington has a similar effect, as does the Wailing Wall in Jerusalem.

In comparison to other stone structures in the world, the Wailing Wall really isn't all that remarkable; a few hundred feet or so of stone blocks rising forty feet in the air, all that remains of the Jewish temple destroyed by the Romans in 70 A.D. Extending twenty feet below ground lies more wall, some of the structure dating back three thousand years to Solomon's Temple. Here, from as early as the eighth century A.D., Jews have come to touch base with tradition and remember their sufferings.

I remember seeing the Wailing Wall for the first time. It was early morning, the beige rock seemed almost soft in the morning sun. Bearded figures had gathered near the base, some with prayer books open, their bodies swaying back and forth, in the peculiar movement known as "shuckling." I learned later that *shuckle* in low German means "to rock." In Yiddish, it has come to describe a manner of praying. A soldier, automatic rifle slung on his back, leaned forward, forehead and upraised hands pressed against the stone. Several men joined hands and danced, twisting and turning, chanting some haunting melody. Off to one side there was a wedding in progress. Further on a bar mitzvah. After their hundred mile march, army recruits will end the ordeal here with a celebration.

All gather at the Wailing Wall, rock named for good reason.

Jerusalem has been destroyed and rebuilt fifteen — or is it eighteen — times. Another one or two hardly seems to matter. Eighteen massacres, eighteen burnings, eighteen re-buildings. What does destruction mean? Yesterday, a man on the radio said that he had once thought of gathering a Christian, a Moslem, and a Jewish fanatic, and having them blow up every holy site in Jerusalem, putting an end to the struggle for possession of the city. But then, he said, the struggle would continue as to who owned the craters, and which rocks were the holiest.

Of all the things that impressed me about the Wailing Wall, one piece of trivia stands out: the cracks. At first glance, it would seem the wall is one solid surface. But up close you can see minute spaces where bits of foliage cling to life. And in the cracks rest scraps of paper. After a time, you discover the source. Jews and tourists alike pause, and rummage for a pen and notepad. They write, fold the paper, then stuff it in a crack. In Italy, there would be vendors selling pens and paper, even prayers already written.

I don't remember what I wrote. It wasn't a complaint at life's injustices or a plea for my enemies' destruction. Nor the lingering thought that all is straw. The stones of the Wailing Wall change everything.


Our stone arrived at its new home safely. To unload it we tied it to the poplar in the backyard and drove away. The stone landed with a thump, settling into the dirt as if, after a few million years elsewhere, this was its intended destination. Norma will plant ground cover around it. It will be a cool place to go to on a hot afternoon. A place to rest and watch the lake. Take turns perhaps.

Of course, it won't happen. Once a year at most. Too hard and too uncomfortable. Just as it was fifty years ago. And yet ...

Here at the lake you realize that time seems to be a great monster. What do you do with it? How do you feed it? Houses are bought and sold in the space of a year. People move away. Nothing to do. Too far from town. Summer comes; the toys accumulate and the activities become more anxious. Between May and August I built two pergolas and a brick walk.

It's as if one can escape time in the shelter of things. Not that there's anything wrong with pergolas. Or even the neighbours snow-mobile, although that's a bit hard to admit. It's just that you can expect too much of them.

Somehow a stone is different. But not any stone. Rather one you can hold in your hand and hear voices with. Or sit on. With cracks and spaces, a place to run your fingers over and remember all that's written there.

# the night God played at Danceland

*I just wanted to go over with you some of the announcements of what's happening in our church this week, and on into the fall. I've printed out the ones I am aware of. I'm sure there are more and if you have one, feel free to offer it. It is so important to remember that our life together here is truly participatory. Let's just go over them together before we begin.*

The words ooze out of her for several minutes as she explains each announcement from several different angles. While she speaks, she continues adjusting the microphone arm, up an inch, down a little, a slight move to the side; an elaborate performance much like that of a keynote speaker who takes several drinks of water before beginning, then lights his pipe, all the while studying his notes. I begin to be suspicious that this could be that old device of the preacher which I have used myself. Finding I have little to say or doubting what I have prepared, I fill up the space in whatever way I can, words being the most convenient means.

Her vestments do nothing to ease my doubts: the robe, with enough cloth for two, topped off with a stole and a cross too large by a half remind me of a woman who puts on more and more makeup in hopes of finally looking beautiful. But it's not just the fumbling and the words; it's the sound, a practiced mellowness, each word carefully chosen, the voice of the understanding pastor, the all caring therapist, and the mother who is never too burdened to care.

When I arrive home at the end of the week I will tell my wife what happened, and she will say, "Why did you go in the first place? You knew what you would find."

But I'm here, second pew from the back, way over on the side. Maybe once every six months I make another stab at going to church, often when I'm away from home. The old church, like so many of its kind, with its bricks, stained glass windows and hardwood floors, shiny with a new coat of varnish, has a kind comfort to it. I like wandering in alone, escaping the greeters at the door who are determined to welcome me whether I want it or not, and watching the old women in the corner peeking over their glasses, whispering to one another, wondering who I am.

There's no shortage of seats. Of the twenty or so people scattered about, most are over sixty and some well beyond. A sense of tranquility hangs over the scene, maybe a little sadness: older folk, chatting and announcing, in spite of themselves and whatever the preacher is saying, that the most active part of this church's life for the foreseeable future will be funerals.

I hunker down, my back wedged against the corner of the pew, knowing I can daydream through the worst of it, sleep if need be.

*So let us begin with the call to worship. But before we do that maybe we should just look at the hymns. Two of them may not be familiar to us, so I'm just going to ask the organist to play each one through and we can listen to it. Then we can try singing it just for practice. Don't hold back; just fill your lungs and sing right out. I'll ask the organist to just play the first one, No. 374. The sentiment of this hymn is just beautiful.*

I have come to church, if not with the highest expectations, at least with what I thought were good reasons. After five days at writer's school, a time in which I have gone from a state of high anticipation to despair and back to a place of quiet gratitude, I wanted to come to church. I wanted to confess my sins. Not the little ones, an argument here, a made-an-ass-of-myself there. If that's as bad as it gets, who cares? Least of all God. I wanted to confess the growing self-doubt, the fear that whatever

I was trying to write was all straw, the confession of a leper who has put himself outside the camp, only to be called back and given a place at the table. More than confession, then, I wanted to give thanks. I wanted to belt out an old hymn. Hear a word. Hear Mary's song.

My soul magnifies the Lord,
and my spirit rejoices in God my
Saviour
for he has regarded the low estate
of his handmaiden.
For behold, henceforth all generations
will call me blessed;
for he who is mighty has done great
things for me
and holy is his name.

*The version of the Lord's Prayer we will be using today is printed for you. Maybe we should just go over it because it may come as something of a shock for us when we have been used to a more traditional version. I picked this version up at a workshop I attended last fall. The leader, a Jewish scholar, told us that this prayer would have sounded quite different in its original Hebrew. This version is probably closer to the original. Let me just read it over for you, and then you can join in. I'm sure in time you'll get a better feel for it.*

No improvement there. My mind begins to wander as I remember the band I heard a week before at Danceland, but I stop myself, a voice from within pleading her case. Give her time. There's still hope; the readings could save her. Surely, she can find some inspiration in Hosea, the broken prophet, the man whose wife went chasing after men while he goes into the streets to bring her back. He looks at his Israel and says that God has taken it back, when Israel has gone whoring after other gods. Or the story from Luke. A farmer builds bigger and bigger barns to house his crops. In his wealth, he says to his soul, "Take your ease, eat, drink, and be merry." But God says, "Fool! This night your soul is required of you." A preacher's dream.

Danceland, built on the shore of Little Manitou Lake, Saskatchewan in 1928, boasts a 5000 sq. ft. hardwood dance floor riding on a cushion of bound horsehair.

*In my sermon this morning I want to reflect for a few minutes on the break-in that occurred last week at our church. I haven't the full report yet, but it appears that locks were broken and a cabinet forced open as the thief looked for money that wasn't there. As I said, I haven't the full report, but I want to say to the thief that if he had come at any other time during the day, or if he was here with us now, surely we could show him treasures far greater than any money he could have found. There's the picture above the communion table ... eighty years old ... cup and paten in the cupboard ... stained glass windows ...*

Danceland. I can't believe what my eyes are telling me. The hardwood floor is moving, an almost imperceptible rising and falling as the dancers swing past, propelled by the beat of Frank Ball's band playing the "Beer Barrel Polka."

"Horsehair," shouts an old timer from across the table. "Horse hair under there."

"Horsehair?"

"Sure ... that's what makes it move. Balls of horsehair bound up tight and laid under there with the hardwood riding on top. Best damn dance floor in Canada. The floor gives a little. You can dance all night and your legs won't get tired."

The music stops and the dancers find their tables while the band rearranges itself for another charge. Frank steps aside and lets his son take over on the accordion. He gets right into it, an old time waltz. This kid can play — maybe better than his old man. Then the soloist takes over.

> One day at a time sweet Jesus
> That's all I'm asking of you
> Just for today help me to say
> One day at a time.

The words float out across the hall, up into the rafters and back, a sound that moves inside your body so you can't sit down. I wave to Joan for a dance — not my wife, but that doesn't matter. We dance, turning and turning. And I decide I can help the soloist.

> Yesterday's gone sweet Jesus
> And tomorrow may never be mine
> Just for today, help me to say
> One day at a time

*But I want to say to the thief that even if he took from us the windows, our pictures , the paten, there remains a treasure that can never be stolen. There remains the love and concern of the people. I want him to come here and see this, and receive it for himself, a treasure that cannot be stolen or confined to a building, but one that is given away.*

I sink back in my pew, her voice droning on.Suddenly, I see before me a courtroom with a trial in progress. To my astonishment the defendant in the dock is none other than the preacher I have been listening to all morning. The plaintiff I do not recognize.

*Judge:* You, Reverend, stand accused of the most serious of offences. Not only are you charged with groping and fondling within your congregation, an activity in which some seem to have willingly participated, you are charged by God himself with having groped and fondled Him on August 2, in the year of our Lord 1998, between the hours of 10:30 and 11:30 a.m. and on many such occasions in the years preceding. How do you plead?

*Defendant:* I have no idea what you mean. I have never laid a hand on anyone, let alone God.

*Judge:* These are most serious charges. God, as the plaintiff in this case, have you any evidence to support your accusations?

*God:* I most certainly do. She whispers in my ear and snuggles up to me in church. It's not so much what she does, in fact, she has never really touched me. It's the intent, the tone of her voice. I feel I am being violated at an emotional level. But that's not the worst of it. I keep waiting for something to happen, wanting something more. Oh, this sounds terrible. But we never get anywhere, I just end up frustrated. And how would you feel, Your Honour, if we came into your court and never once mentioned your name. What's more she told my favourite reading — the story of the farmer who builds bigger barns so as to store up all his grain — but never even mentioned what I said! I told him, "Fool this night your soul is required of you." That's a bit harsh, I know, but don't you think it's rather good? Yet, when she was done telling the story, the whole thing was like a tomato run through a blender.

*Judge:* Reverend, what have you to say for yourself?

*Defendant:* I am outraged. How dare He, God that is, even suggest such nonsense? I have no idea what He means.

*Judge:* Ignorance is no defence, and I do find the plaintiff believable. I will have to find you guilty as charged. Do you have anyone to speak on your behalf?

A silence hangs over the courtroom. Then I hear myself say, "I will speak for her."

*Judge:* Who are you?

*Witness:* I was there. I saw and heard what happened. God is not wrong in His charges; those things of which He speaks did occur. But is there not room for mercy if the defendant did only what she knew? Where were those who trained her? Where were those who should know better, her elders and teachers, those in the seminary and head office? And above all, where was God? I'm not sure what God is complaining about; I question whether He was even there last Sunday morning.

*Judge:* How can you be so sure God was not there?

*Witness:* I saw Him at Danceland, heard him up there in Frank Ball's orchestra playing the accordion. And Jesus was on the sax and the Spirit was singing. I was there and sang, too. This woman had to be alone in her church.

*Judge:* God, is the testimony of this witness true?

*God:* I hadn't realized ...

*Judge:* Ignorance is no defence.

*Witness:* Your Honour, there's more to it. There's a woman I know, a Ukrainian baba who wants more than anything else to go to church on a Sunday morning and find a little life and colour, robes and crosses and incense. To lift up her voice, and to be lifted up. And what does she get? Leftovers, three days old and cold. And there's my friend — he wants to go to mass, stand in line, and see the bread broken, and the cup passed. But he's divorced and married to an Anglican. She would like to find a priest with a little life, not one who wound up twenty years ago and has all but ground to a halt, saying the same words, wearing vestments that smell of old sweat. And there's my wife who has given up, and stays in the garden on Sunday morning. And there's me who just wants to remember how I screwed it all up, but now I can sing.

*Judge:* The charge is that you have been absent God. You have left this pastor and her people alone and have gone to Danceland. Is that true?

*God:* I hadn't thought of it like that. But now that you mention it, I guess it's true.

*Judge:* Reverend, under the law you are guilty. But given the extenuating circumstances, I will stay the charges, giving you time to rehabilitate yourself. You will be present at Danceland every Saturday night until 2 a.m. for the next three years. As for you, God, the matter is quite different. You have abandoned your church, an extreme dereliction of duty. What have you to say?

God says nothing for a time, then rises slowly to His feet and stands before the judge.

*God:* Your Honour, you have decided well. But, in all respect, hear me once more. Hear me all of you. I am not coming back. I am staying at Danceland. I am sorry. I don't expect you to understand this or what is to follow. But I am not coming back. All I can offer is an invitation. On Saturday, August 12, at nine o'clock Frank Ball is playing at Danceland. His son will play accordion and his wife will sing solo. I want you to come. I'm learning how to dance again. I would be glad to teach you what I've learned.

*Judge:* Reverend, and all you gathered here, I can say nothing more than to remind you, you have received an invitation. Case adjourned.

*And so if that thief is out there somewhere and can hear me, I would like to say to him: You should come in the daytime, come on a Sunday to see and receive the fellowship and warmth of this church. This is its true treasure, one you cannot steal from us.*

# at the jazz concert

like thunder from a prairie storm
the bass dog rumbles
    sending tremors racing
   through stones and aging wood.
the lead cat, as if possessed,
  attacks the piano, hurling
    Jesus,   Jesus,  Jesus
into the pulpit, pews, balcony.
mid the chaos the drummer weeps,
  brush strokes whispering,
  deep calling unto deep.

amid the devastation
an old man remembers
his best years are gone.
shivers in his belly
  as if once more he holds
   a woman in his arms,
    or stands alone
at the edge of endless prairie
  awed by the swelling
  of a stubborn rhythm
    demanding birth.

# they come in threes

In my memory weddings are but a blur of gowns, receptions, and rented tuxedos, the same food and the same jokes. However, I can tell you
the details of any number of funerals.

Don't get me wrong; weddings are necessary and the odd one has
even proven memorable. I would put my own in that category,
although there was nothing exceptional about it. In keeping with the
tradition of small towns, there was a rehearsal the night before where
the preacher put us through our paces. The next day everything went
as planned; no one flubbed their lines. The sun was shining and many
good people joined us to celebrate. We had dinner in the town hall;
the women of the community served overdone roast beef with peas and
carrots, and apple pie for dessert. An uncle toasted the bride, and I
reciprocated. Norma and I stood in front of the cake with a knife
poised, while countless pictures were taken. Then one of the women
cut up the cake and we walked around handing out little pieces to all
the guests. At some point Norma changed from her gown into her travelling outfit. During dinner, someone had jacked up the rear wheels of
our car. We couldn't make our grand exit until the perpetrators — two
brothers-in-law — removed the jack and set us free.

It was a good wedding — I'm glad I did it; but it was predictable,
as weddings generally are. Maybe it's the tinkling of glasses until the
bride kisses the groom, until the parents kiss one another, until the
bride kisses the best man, and on and on until every kissing combina-

tion has been exhausted. Or perhaps it's a lingering irritation from the weddings I have conducted, thinking I should have been paid at least as much as the cost of the bride's gown or half the liquor bill. Occasionally, I have felt as though I was at the whim and fancy of the bride and her mother, and was required, like the train of the gown, to bring up the rear.

Funerals are different. No cakes. No rehearsals. Happiness is not the objective, and tears outnumber kisses. There's a finality, an inevitability in the air — yet you can never be quite sure what's going to happen, or what memories will remain. Memories which return with feelings that are beyond sadness or pleasure.


I can still see my grandfather lying in his coffin, an old man with a grey moustache, hands crossed, asleep. The sterilization of death having not yet reached our little town, the coffin and body remained in the bedroom where friends stopped by to view the body and then to visit, a celebration of life before it became a fad. It was taken for granted that children be involved. Mrs. Jarvis, the matriarch who, as circumstances required, filled the role of midwife, nurse, and counsellor to the community, took my cousin and I into the bedroom and lifted each of us up to make sure we could see. One red rose, a real one, pinned to the satin of the coffin, rested directly over the folded hands when the lid was closed. Soon after his death my grandmother died, and I remember my father standing in the church, his tweed cap in his hand, staring at the ceiling. I am sure he wanted to cry, but didn't. It was as close to tears as I ever saw him.

Of course, not everything that happens around deaths and funerals is tragic and sad.


When Little Jake died, he had no family and little money, so they laid him out in the partially built house of a neighbour. Here Father and three others, undertakers for the day, prepared Jake for burial. As was customary on such occasions, they stopped for a drink to fortify themselves for the task ahead. It was reported that one of the men, Frank Pavelich, opened a bottle, held it up, and called out, "Jake, do you want a beer?" Receiving no answer, he is supposed to have said, "For sure Jake's dead; he never turned down a beer."

My father proceeded with the shaving, assured by another man that he need not worry about cutting Jake's face or drawing blood. One of the problems they did encountered was getting Jake into his suit. The pants went on easily enough, but they couldn't get Jake, stiff as he was, into his jacket. After some discussion, it was decided to cut the jacket in half with a pair of tin snips. They then slipped it on, one half at a time, pinning the pieces together with shingle nails. As a finishing touch, they slipped a fresh package of Snuss, which Jake was known to like, inside his vest pocket.

Along with the tragedy and gallows humour, there have been other occasions, times marked by simplicity and grace, where, to my surprise, I have been deeply touched by the death and the funeral that followed.

I had been in the parish about two months and was out in the countryside, a shepherd looking for sheep that belonged to me, but instead finding quite a few that didn't belong to anyone. As I departed from one home, the farmer pointed to a grove of trees in the distance.

"You should stop in there. Two boys and their parents. No one sees too much of them. I hear the old man has been sick."

Following directions, I drove down a side road that gradually deteriorated into a trail, which led to a grove of poplars and a farm. There was no sign of life, but I knocked on the door and waited. Everything from the junk machinery to the weather-beaten house to the timid dog, that looked at me and crawled under the porch, seemed in the grip of a deep sadness. Finally, the door opened just far enough that I could see the wrinkled face of an old woman, hair pulled back in a bun — a Ma Kettle squinting at me through wire rimmed glasses.

"Yes, what's it you want?"

Introducing myself, I said I was the new minister in town.

"What's that?"

"I'm the new preacher." I have always found such introductions difficult; you can never be sure what title people will understand: priest,
preacher, minister, padre. Anglicans say rector, which to me always
sounds just slightly naughty and suggestive. In a hospital, I once intro-
duced myself as the chaplain to a patient who was hard of hearing. In a
creaky voice he replied, "Chaplain? Only Chaplain I ever knew was
Charlie." The nurses in the nearby station found it all very amusing.

This time I was in luck. The old woman's face brightened and the
door swung open.

"Oh, I heard there was a new one. Anderson's our name. Come on
in ... we haven't had a preacher here in years." Then, almost in a whisper, she said, "And maybe it's good you came now."

Once inside, I was met by two figures who I assumed were "the
boys" — grown men, both of them were well over fifty years of age.
One, a slight-built individual as timid looking and forlorn as the dog I
had met earlier, stared at me, then stepped forward, shook hands and
offered a squeaky "Hello."

"Morley's his name," the old woman announced. "This here's
Harry."

Harry, in contrast to his brother, must have weighed over 200
pounds. With his hands tucked in the front of his high bib overalls, he
peered at me from behind a three-day whisker with the expression of a
mischievous schoolboy. He offered a friendly "Hello" from where he
was standing. If there was a man of the house it appeared to be Morley.

I was led at once to a cot in the corner of the room where a figure
lay huddled under a blanket. "This is the new preacher, Arthur. Can
you hear me? This is my husband; he's not well." In a low voice the old
woman went on to tell me he had been diagnosed with mouth cancer.
"But Arthur has been Liberal all his life and he swore he wouldn't have
any part of the medicare the government brought in. He refuses to go
for treatment."

I couldn't believe anyone could be so stubborn — and foolish. My
father had voted Liberal all his life; while he looked upon the CCF
with utter contempt, he had seen too much sickness coupled with the
fear of not being able to afford a doctor that even he gave the social-
ists credit for medicare. I suspected that this poor soul's real reason for

refusing to see a doctor had more to do with fear than politics. Nevertheless, there he lay, the side of his mouth an open wound, which he wiped from time to time with a wadded handkerchief; it was all I could do to breathe the air and look at him. He tried to speak, but his words were slurred.

"What do you think we should do?" The old woman looked at me, a bewildered look on her face.

"You haven't seen a doctor?"

"Not since we got the diagnosis."

"I'd call the ambulance and take him to the hospital." A higher authority than her husband had given her permission to act.

"That's what we'll do. Morley, you call the ambulance."

Without hesitation, Morley went to the phone, one of the old crank affairs on the wall, and called the local funeral home, which also operated the ambulance service. It had been an afternoon of surprises, and I was in for another. As Morley spoke, in a voice somewhat lower in tone than I expected, he suddenly switched in mid-sentence to a high falsetto, not unlike that of Tiny Tim singing "Tip Toe Through The Tulips." Then, just as suddenly, his voice dropped to its original deep bass. On the conversation went, Morley switching from low to squeak and back. I remember wondering what the receptionist must have been thinking on the other end of the line. In the four years I was in the community, I never became accustomed to Morley's voice. Each time we met I would find myself staring at him, waiting for him to hit a high C without warning.

In less than an hour the ambulance arrived, and the old man was taken to the hospital. He died two weeks later. At the funeral, Harry and Morley, dressed in suits that didn't quite fit, sat in the front row. Between them sat their mother, wearing her best dress and a high, round hat with flowers on one side, a splendid creation that I assumed had been in style forty years before. Normally, I can go through a funeral and not be too affected by what's going on, or at least keep control and do what is required. But looking at the boys and their wisp of a mother, I had to stop in the midst of things and gather myself before I could go on.

I know funerals can be quite awful — the preacher makes a saint out of the deceased although everyone knows it isn't true or the music is bad or there are three eulogies when one would have been too many. But the event itself — a coffin and body, the long trip to the graveyard, the words of committal, lowering the coffin, filling the grave — has a way of stopping the merry-go-round just for a moment.

Of course, I attend a lot more funerals these days than weddings. There have been three deaths in our circle of friends in the past ten days. I was reminded of my childhood and an old Scottish lady, Maggie we called her, who believed that deaths came in threes. If there was one, there would be two more. No one believed her, of course, but when the second one came, you waited, wondering who would be the third.

I suppose you could say we felt a bit of relief today; we've had our three.

Andy and Maggie McBroom, much loved neighbours of our family. Among other things Maggie was known for her conviction that deaths came in threes.

# peace be with you

Tuesday morning. I have been waiting an hour to call the doctor for an appointment. My urinary system is acting up; blood in my urine to be exact. Late Friday evening when the problem first appeared, I wanted to find out immediately what was going on. But it was a long weekend and there was nothing to do but wait.

The interesting thing, and I have seen this before but never stopped to look at the reaction carefully, is the sequence of emotions that occurred as I waited. Initially, there was fear. I could feel it in the pit of my stomach and there wasn't much I could do with it. My "emotional immune system" had not yet kicked in.

I feared what might be wrong, imagining at once that I had cancer. This simply served to remind me of my long-standing fear of the medical system, which often finds expression in criticism. I fear the descent into appointments, tests, waiting, conflicting opinions, and the nagging suspicion that no one knows what the hell they are doing. And I fear myself, fear becoming docile, following any old shepherd that shows up. Then I begin to fear that these feelings might remain, that I will not know joy again. Quite irrational, I tell myself. Yes, but there are times when reason is such a feeble thing.

All day Saturday I had no will to do anything, a condition made all the worse by the intense heat. By three in the afternoon it had reached 38°C. I sat down and tried to read. The author had suffered terribly at the hands of thugs who run various parts of Latin America. One writes in order to bear the grief. Compared to his story, a little blood in my urine doesn't seem like much. But it is my blood. In the wrong place.

In the evening, we went out for dinner with some friends to celebrate our anniversary. The wine and food helped a little, but it was a rather subdued party. I have noticed in the past that the effect of alcohol, to a considerable degree, depends on my mood. Perhaps the others felt it was a party, but I knew I was dragging, the wine failing to lift my spirits.

On the third day, I proposed to Norma that we go for a drive. She agreed without asking where we will go; she already knows. We headed about thirty miles southeast through rough country on gravel roads until we came to the hills, the place where my parents farmed and where I grew up. We stopped at the lake where my parents' ashes are scattered. Then we drove past the old farm and stopped at the site of the school I attended, now no more than two acres of grass marked by a fading sign. Last year, I spent a month refinishing the sign, sanding it and painting it in bright red and white enamel: Chatham School No. 3117. Some day the ground will be cultivated and seeded but for now it remains a schoolyard.

The trip varies a little. We stopped at two sloughs where Norma cut bundles of cattails for an arrangement she was planning. In midafternoon we arrived at my cousin's farm and stopped for a visit, the kind of thing you are meant to do in the country. They welcomed us, apologizing for the smell that drifted from the direction of the barn, where the corrals were being cleaned. Inside the house, fans were running and the temperature was comfortable. We sipped a cool drink and talked. Grandchildren were well. A daughter-in-law was expecting her second child. Hay must be hauled for the winter. It is cheaper to hire a semi than haul it in your own pickup truck. Inevitably, we get around to another subject that hangs in the air as surely as the odour from the corrals: drought. No one has mentioned it, but you know it's there: a hint of worry in their eyes and a tone of grim determination in their voices. Pasture's burning up. Need rain, bad. Drier than a bird's ass. Even a thunderstorm would help.

For as far back as I can remember I can recall this same conversation. Not a conversation really. It reminds me more of an ancient form of prayer perfected by the Desert Fathers centuries ago, called "arrow" prayers. A word or phrase, uttered or remembered, rises up, aimed in the general direction of God. From the tone of our voices it is evident we have little confidence; the gods of rain are absent. But the prayers must still be offered, if for no other reason that it can't do any harm. When we left, they thank us for stopping by. The smell from the cor-rals seemed to have diminished.


The fourth day and my mood has progressed, at least it has changed. Rather than making plans to build this or that, go to town, spend money, or become preoccupied with some problem or other, it is as if I have stepped off the train and resist going farther. I am watching myself, moving in slow motion. I feel vulnerable and fragile. All my cover has been brushed away to expose depths long denied access.

I notice two things in particular. First, I remember certain friends; I see their faces; I want to be with them. I imagine a table at a sidewalk café. A waitress takes our order for tea and a croissant, and for an hour we are alone, telling old stories over again. Remembering their faces and voices, I have an urge to call them on the phone, but I have learned this would be a mistake. I must not close the distance between us. Instead I will write them, talk out loud to them, remember an inci-dent from years before when we were together and tell it once more. We make love across a room, at a glance. Or across a country by letter.


There is something else that happens, the same response really as remembering old friends, but in a different form; I remember certain poets and writers. They seem to appear as if they have been waiting in the wings. Patrick Kavanaugh. Anton Boisen. Pat Ingoldsby. Kavanaugh was a drunk, Boisen went mad, and Ingoldsby, plagued by cerebral palsy, has spent time in a mental hospital. Why remember these old, broken down poets and preachers? For the same reason I remember my friends. No axes to grind. No bodies to be nailed to the cross one more time. None of them were really successful. Kavanaugh attained some recognition as a poet, but died a drunk, saying that com-ing to Dublin was the greatest mistake of his life. Likewise with Boisen;

he succeeded to a certain point, but remained a misfit. Ingoldsby? I would expect this is the only place you will ever see his name in print. He may be known in Ireland where they have more room for misfits.

I heard Pat read his poetry one evening in Ireland at a literary festival in the village of Carlow. The evening before we had witnessed one of Ireland's leading poets, Paul Durcan, perform his poetry. Standing at the microphone, solemn faced, twisting his neck and shoulders as if in pain, staring upward into the rafters of the ceiling, Durcan stood there saying nothing. When finally he spoke, the words were as strained and twisted as his body. His books were on sale, the latest being two glossy volumes commissioned by authorities in England and Ireland. Durcan's poetry isn't bad; some of it is very good. But I don't remember it nor have I had any fun with it.

All of this in sharp contrast to Pat Ingoldsby. He limped on to the stage and sat on a stool, smoking one cigarette after another. A lot of what he read was not very good, made all the worse by his inept attempts to be funny. He had one book for sale, a slim volume which he had self-published by scraping together his meagre savings and borrowing from the bank. But I remember his poetry. Only Pat could write about being all alone in his house sewing on a button. Or about a vagina set loose in the Vatican. There's a communion to his poems, a broken loneliness that gives way to joyful defiance, something a man needs if he's going to make it.


The doctor's office opened at nine. I called and the nurse asked me what the problem was. As carefully as I could, I told her there was something wrong with my water works and she understood.

"See you at two. Bring a urine sample."

By three I have seen the doctor. He has done the usual and concluded there is nothing to worry about. "Just the after effects of the operation. It will happen from time to time."

On the way home I stop at the liquor store and buy a good bottle of wine for dinner.

# why is it the good ones go first?

"We want you to come."

The voice, which bears an unmistakable Cree accent, is that of a slight built young man in jeans and leather jacket. He has appeared outside the door of my shack with two others, all of whom I have seen about town, but do not know by name.

"Come with you? I'm not sure what you mean," I reply, looking down at them from the doorway of my shack. Apart from passing in the street and an occasional greeting, I have had little to do with the people of the reserve, nameless figures referred to only as "they" and "them." It is a story of long standing, embarrassing if you have time to think about it.

Even though I have lived in close proximity to native people all my life, I know more about Arabs and Africans than I do of these men. Later, I will admit to myself that, up until this summer, I have had but two brief experiences with Indians, both of them no more than fragments of memory.

My father spoke of an incident occurring in 1922. Three Indians arrived in town, driving one white horse pulling a stone boat, a contraption of planks on skids used for hauling stones and anything else that needed moving. They were looking for work from the settlers, picking stones from the same land their ancestors had hunted on. No one gave them work, and Father didn't know where they went, or what became of them.

Then there were the two men in dark hats, braids down their backs, leaning on the rail by the train station. My nose pressed against the window of the car I stared at them. They were smoking cigarettes. Quiet, mysterious figures. I asked my mother who they were. Indians, she said. What are they doing? Waiting for the train. Where do they come from? The reserve.

"The funeral ... we want you to come," the leader of the trio replies. He glances up at me for a moment, his face expressionless except for the intensity of his brown, deep set eyes.

What the hell is he talking about? I know there's a funeral in the afternoon, but Jimmy Bear was Anglican and the local priest has the funeral. Why do they want me, a white man from the outside, for whom both the natives and the Anglican Prayer Book remain a mystery?

"Are you sure you want me?" I try to look as confused as possible, hoping to convince them they have the wrong man.

"Yes ... we want you to speak, say some words, like before." The others nod in agreement. Again our eyes meet for an instant.

Like before. So that's it. They want me there because of the other funeral. Six weeks previous a white man, one of the old outfitters and leading citizens of the town, died from liver failure brought on by drinking too much whisky over too many years. He, too, had been Anglican, but the new Anglican priest had not yet arrived. Would I take the funeral? A preacher, any preacher would do. Although nervous about the Anglican liturgy, I agreed to take the service.

I prepared for the funeral, but at the last minute the new Anglican priest appeared and took over. He invited me to assist, which I did, reading a lesson and speaking for a few minutes. The funeral was an impressive affair. A large black hearse, chrome polished and glinting in the sun carried the oak casket back south. There were two grey cars as well, more sleek than the hearse, to take the family and pallbearers from the church to the town hall for lunch. When the hearse and limousines drove down Main Street, with most of the cars in town strung out behind, they created a sight as impressive as a visit from the prime minister.

"Is it all right with the priest?" I ask, hoping this might save me.

"Yes, we told him already." The voice has a quiet determination about it. As determined as the eyes.

"You're sure you want me to come then?"

"Yes. You spoke good at the other one."

"Then I will come." The delegation nods its thanks and leaves.

Back in my cabin, I sit down to think over what I will say. Jimmy, only twenty-four years old, drowned in the lake earlier in the week. Given that one brother was in jail and another drank too much, the general opinion on coffee row was that Jimmy was the best man in the family. His death has hit the community hard.

What do Indians do at funerals? I see the face and the eyes of the young man at my door, a poker player's eyes that give nothing away. What do I say? As a last resort I begin pacing about the room, talking to myself, looking for words.

"Talking to those three ... that's the longest conversation you've had with an Indian in your life. What could you possibly have to say? Nothing. Yes, but they did ask."

I am interrupted by a voice from outside the door. "Hey ... who you talkin' to in there? Open up. Brought you some fresh water."

"Mike," I holler, flinging open the door, "what do Indians do at funerals? What am I to say?"

Mike has lived here for years, hauling fresh water from the river to supply the families of the town. He is an "escapee," as he describes himself, one of several such people in town who have fled the south for various reasons, alcohol appearing to be the main one. The north, of course, cured nothing, and Mike's problems grew steadily worse until even he became frightened. After a particularly bad drinking bout he packed up his pyjamas, toothbrush, and a bottle of beer, and presented himself at the doctor's office. "I'm a drunk, Doc. You gotta do something." With that he drank the beer and checked himself into the hospital. He has been sober ever since, and is one of the few people in town I trust.

"They want you to speak?" Mike squints at me. "Must like you or they wouldn't have asked. Just do what you'd do for anybody else. Keep it short and sit down. You'll be okay."

The old priest and I meet in the vestry. He reassures me all will go well, then offers a brief prayer before we take our places. Although I have been in this church before, I am still uncomfortable. The platform rises two feet above the main floor, leaving me with the feeling that I must look like an owl perched on a stump. But only when I risk looking out at the congregation is the shock complete.

A mass of solemn brown faces stare up at me, every seat filled. Men crowd in at the back and stand in the aisle halfway to the front. Several women, in black dresses and shawls, weep softly in the front row. Before the altar, on two wooden blocks, rests the coffin. It's a plywood box, constructed by one of the men of the community, wider at the point of a man's shoulders, tapered to both ends and finished with black cotton cloth. No handles, no chrome. A single vase of wild lilies stands in the centre of the coffin. Something — perhaps the simplicity of it all coupled with the stark black of the coffin — casts a spell, and for a time we seem suspended, unmoving.

The organist, an old woman only slightly younger than the pump organ itself, commences playing "What A Friend We Have In Jesus" and the people follow. I remain silent. I know the hymn, have sung it countless times, but I have never heard this sound before: a wailing lament like the drone of the pipes, rising to the rafters and returning, wafting through the open windows, out onto the lake and beyond, carrying the grief of a hundred souls. No cathedral organ, no massed choir of medieval monks could compare to this haunting chant. We reach the end and close with a long, plaintive Amen.

Silence. In the distance a magpie shrieks. The old priest rises, a frail figure who, it seems, might well collapse under the weight of his robes. "Lord, let me know mine end, and the number of my days," he begins, droning on through the prayers in a high-pitched, brittle voice. There follows another hymn, this time with several verses and a chorus; it is played and sung at the same measured pace as the first. By the time my turn arrives everything I have prepared seems out of place, an intrusion. Instead, I thank them for inviting me, say a few words about the loss of a son and brother, and sit down. After almost an hour, the service draws to a close.

72

I decide I am not needed at the cemetery and begin making my way back to my shack, relaxed that my part is over. I can even allow myself to admit I am pleased I was invited.

"Nobody to drive. Will you do it?"

A pallbearer, one of the same men I met earlier in the day, runs up to me with a set of keys in his hand. The hearse, a battered station wagon belonging to one of the outfitters and used for every odd job in town, has no driver.

"OK ... where ..." Before I can ask questions the keys are thrust into my hand and the man rushes off to tend to the coffin. I find the station wagon and take my place at the wheel. As I sit there a peculiar sensation begins to take over, something for which I have no name. It has come before. Like the time I went downhill skiing for the first time. After struggling for an hour by the ski lodge I said to hell with it and managed to get on the lift. I went all the way to the top, over the most beautiful mountain I had ever seen. Dumped in a heap, I gathered myself and started down. And then it happened; a kind of laughing broke out deep inside. A feeling of being out on the edge, carried by the mountain, the sun, and the snow. Everything clear, and sharp. No time to plan for an outcome. Happy? No, happy isn't the right word. Something else.

Hearse driver. That's it. You've never been a hearse driver. Son, student, preacher, patient. But you have never been a hearse driver before. This may be your calling, I tell myself.

The pallbearers slide the coffin in behind me, the end resting on the open tailgate. I start the motor.

"Wait ... there's no car for the pallbearers," someone shouts.

"Ride in the station wagon," a voice answers. Two men crowd into the front seat with me. Two more crouch over the coffin, along the sides, while two sit on the tail gate.

By God Orville, this thing's going to fly. Told you it would, Wilbur. The laughter rolls on, in full flight.

I slip into low gear and the old, yellow station wagon, with its fenders rusted and muffler half gone, moves down the dusty street. In the mirror, I can see a procession of half-tons and battered cars forming up behind. Small groups of women and children crowd the edge of the road. Three dogs join in. How fine we must look. *Ride on, ride on in majesty, in lowly pomp ride on.* Once at the cemetery, the men hoist the coffin to their shoulders and carry it to the grave.

Another crisis; no one has thought of a rope to lower the coffin. In the station wagon we find a length of old rope, discarded from an anchor for one of the lake boats. Looping a piece under each end of the coffin, the men ease the frail box out over the grave where it hangs suspended. Solemnly, the old priest takes his place at the head of the grave.

"Forasmuch as it has pleased Almighty God to take unto himself the soul of our brother here departed ..."

Crash. The rope snaps, dropping one end of the coffin into the grave, the other end left angled in the air. The box hangs, suspended, looking like a torpedoed ship about to sink beneath the waves. Someone produces a knife and cuts the rope, the coffin falls to the bottom.

"... we therefore commit his body to the ground, earth to earth, ashes to ashes, dust to dust."


I walk back toward the car as the men set about filling in the grave. My laughter, if that is what it is, has subsided, as it always does, and in its place has come a sadness that I do not understand. On the bridge I am met by Jimmy's sister, a young woman, shy but attractive in her black dress. She thanks me for all I have done.

"Why is it," she asks, "that the good ones always go first?"

I have dreaded such questions because preachers, especially young ones, assume they have answers. But today on the bridge something is different.

"I don't know." No other words come, and she asks for nothing more.

We stand for a moment watching the river tumbling over the rocks, then turn and together walk back across the bridge.

# trick or treat

In the front window a pumpkin peers into the night. From beyond children's voices pierce the darkness. My children, adults now, sit with my wife and I around our oak dining table.

"Remember the costumes we had ... that time I was Batman and you were a cat?" my son says.

"Yeah," laughs my daughter, "and pillow cases half-full of candy. Some people gave really great things, but those little boxes of raisins ... I threw them in the alley,"

"Did you know that this is All Hallows Eve and tomorrow is All Saints?" I am unsure of myself, but I want them to know our history and tradition, something I have paid little heed to over the years. "It is a time to remember the dead. If there is anyone who comes to mind, family or friends, we could name them. We never did this when I was a kid, but the older I get it seems ... "

I feel awkward. For a moment we sit, silent, four faces caught in the candle's uneven light.

"I wish Grandma were here tonight." There is a note of sadness in my daughter's voice, then a quiet laugh. "Perhaps she is, sitting there in her place at the end of the table." Then my son remembers his grandfather; my wife names her mother. I lean back in my chair; they know what I am talking about.

"I had a brother," I tell them, "who was born before me, but died at birth. I have known about him for years, but have never talked about him." This lost brother, like other pieces of my family history, has remained hidden beneath a shroud of silence. But tonight with a candle, an oak table, and spirits abroad, the shroud has lifted a bit. I have permission to speak about him.

"One time when I was about fourteen I was up at Mrs. Fountain's. She lived on a farm east of us and had some nurse's training before she was married. Out there in the hills she was the person you went to for help. She knew every family, all their ailments and whatever else might be hidden in the closet. I was at her house playing Norwegian Whist with our hired man; Mother and Father were not there. We were talking about some event concerning my family that had occurred prior to my birth. Mrs. Fountain said, 'That was before the baby died.'

"She had to be referring to a baby that had been born into my family. I must have looked surprised because she glanced quickly at her husband and changed the subject. I didn't say any more. I don't know why I didn't ask for details at home, but I never did. Years later I learned more.

"In '65 when we went to the States, I needed a birth certificate to get a visa. Rather than a card with your name, you received a transcript of the original document with the names of your entire family on it. At the head of the list, in my father's handwriting, was my brother's name and then my sister's. I'm at the end. But before my name, there is another entry: Baby Boy. There had been a baby, stillborn. He didn't have a name but he was there, third in line.

"A few years ago when your mother and I stopped at the cemetery where your grandparents are buried, we saw, there in the plot beside the larger graves, a small headstone. It just says 'Baby Boy.' That's my brother."

Again there is silence, but I feel as if I have begun to brush away the dust of forty years. I can see a host of questions I have not stopped to ask before. Who was Baby Boy? Why has he been hidden away? What has kept him from being at our table?

For a moment I am angry, angry with my parents for their silence. I want to say to them, "Why have you said nothing all these years? Why the taboo about speaking of an infant dying? Why has the shroud been so firmly drawn — on many things?"

Then the table brightens. On the white cloth it is as if I see my father writing names: my brother's, my sister's, Baby Boy. He pauses a moment and then I see him write again. This time it is my name.

Silence settles over the room. The candle's ragged tip pushes upward, probing the dark. Something begins to stir. A baby. Stillbirth. If my brother had lived would my name be on the list? Would he have completed this table? Was there some intention that I should live and he should not? My mind presses at the shadows, trying to imagine my brother in my place, trying to imagine not being born. I feel unsettled, embarrassed at asking my questions.

More than death lies hidden beneath this shroud. Stillbirth. A beginning and an end. A return to the beginning, to a warm night with a half moon, to the dark hidden places of a woman's body. A return to pleasure, to a man's desire and a woman's longing. A return to sounds. My father and my mother lusting for one another. Issues forever hidden. Forbidden passion. Illicit joy. Now nothing more than a bit of blood and sinew, dead.

Stillbirth. Sex and death. A witch's brew.

# a kind of hope

Coyotes yip somewhere in the shadows. You shiver and then laugh at yourself, remembering when, as a child, you ran in from the dark to escape some imagined pursuer. Tonight you are glad for the company of friends, wine, and the pleasure of food. Braised breast of duck with caramel sauce, salmon, and ribs that everyone says are like none they have ever had before.

Such is an evening at The Hole in the Wall.

Rosemarie and Nelson have run the restaurant for fifteen years. Once an old Texaco gas station, the building was re-modeled and re-finished with tile and adobe in a fashion we associate with the architecture of South America. Nelson had dreamed of such a restaurant and Rosemarie said do it. Recognition came slowly, and then often from afar. Magazines across the country wrote up the establishment as one of the better places to dine in Canada. Joni Mitchell, of music fame, home for a week to open her art display in Saskatoon, drove out for dinner. "You should be in L.A.," she said. Who better to validate us than one of our own who made it big in L.A.?

Those of us who live here take pride in The Hole in the Wall. It's our symbol, our one identifying feature. One village down the highway has a snowman, another a giant prairie lily. Eastern cities have domes and towers. We have a restaurant, a gourmet restaurant on the

The Hole in the Wall, a gourmet restaurant with the farm fields beyond, established at Shields, Saskatchewan by a native of Peru, Nelson Urtega and Rosemarie, a woman from Saskatoon.

edge of the prairie, loved into being by a man from Peru and a woman from Saskatchewan.

Yet, as much as we take pride in the place, there remains an unease, an ambivalence.

Here on the prairie  eating out means a beer and a steak sandwich at the bar, consumed in twenty minutes with a half hour at the VLT's. A meal at The Hole in the Wall takes a whole evening. For some, the thought of several hours spent talking, enjoying food, watching the candle burn down can be more scary than listening to the coyotes.

A kind of indifference sets in. Three hours is too long to spend at a meal. If not the time, then we point to the price. How can you spend forty or fifty dollars just for a meal? No one mentions that we can spend a few thousand for a new snowmobile or Sea-Doo, and then consume hours on them roaring across the lake or up and down the streets of the village. But, of course, cost and time are but the available reasons given for our uncertainty. The fact is, behind these reasons lies a wound, one inflicted generations ago out of deprivation and hardship, an attitude as enduring as the seasons. Even now, though good times have come, succeeding generations remain ambivalent about seemingly little things such as an evening spent over hors d'oeuvres, braised duck, and a bottle of choice wine. Not only do we not do that kind of thing, we are unsure about the people who do.

A meal, like a new combine or snowmobile, is a functional thing. Does it work? How much did it cost? You put a meal away in order to get on with something else — namely work. It's an outlook born a hundred years ago in the days of settlement and reinforced by the Dirty Thirties, where if you had a frying pan and a potato, you had a meal. Some days it seems we have inherited a gene passed on from an age when the hunt failed; all but a few cave dwellers died, leaving only the thrifty folks who live on rabbit stew and hard work. Whatever the source, it's an attitude that can wither the spirit and make it hard, a sin even, to spend money on a meal and enjoy the intimacy that comes with candles and music, fine food and wine.

There's nothing particularly unique in all this. Every group, every tribe and clan, whether they be Greeks on the island of Crete or street smart citizens in New York, have their own expression of what it is to be wary of the stranger and suspicious of anything different. Here in the village, you realize the prairie has imprinted on our soul a particular version of these same human qualities.

But we're still proud of The Hole in the Wall. Joni Mitchell is right: there's something about this place you can't buy in L.A. And it's not just the atmosphere or the food. It's admiration. Or maybe it's a sense of hope that comes from one man's dream and a woman's determination.

I never wanted to run a restaurant but I still dream of a bakery. A small establishment where I could make bread. No cookies or doughnuts or jellied bismarcks. None of that sugar and dough that all looks the same and has that unmistakable bakery flavour. Just bread: straight brown with five kinds of grain, pita with honey for sweetener, plain brown and cinnamon raisin bagels, foccacia rounds, and French loaves slashed on the top as good as they make in Sonoma, California. Maybe cinnamon buns for a change. I could have the bread fresh every morning and ready again at five when people are on their way home from work. I won't do it, of course. Scared the thing will fail, and besides what would people think?

But Nelson and Rosemarie did it. Somewhere they got the idea to run a restaurant. No — more than that. The desire, desire for a little restaurant with a few tables where people could enjoy food and conversation. It's the kind of dream that if you put it away you will dismiss it because it isn't practical, because you wonder what people will think, because there's no money in it, because ... because ... then something gets tired and goes away. Your angel moves on and settles somewhere else, refusing to return.

Nelson and Rosemarie listened to their desire and not to the becauses.

That's why life seems so unfair this week.

We have known for over a year that Rosemarie had been diagnosed with cancer. With the diagnosis came treatments — tests, chemo, radiation. Weeks of waiting, a lull in the storm where muted hope sets in, the kind where you want to believe the treatments are working. Everyone has a story of someone who beat the same cancer fifteen years ago. Prayers are said. But in the back of your mind lurks a shadow, a foreboding you don't want to examine because you know what you thought was hope is really denial.

But without denial there would be no hope. Or maybe hope is a kind of denial, stories you tell yourself to keep going.

Rosemarie did improve, looked her usual self, and was back at work in the restaurant. Then more tests. More waiting. Then came word the cancer had returned. Lungs this time. At best a few months. And no one knows quite what to say or do.

There's a full moon tonight. The kind where you put on your jacket to go out and watch. The fields lie immersed in a strange kind of half-light where you see but don't see. Swaths of grain lie row on row. No sense of distance. Combines, balls of light and dust suspended in the dark, turn and turn. Anxious, in a hurry. Always in a hurry.

And the lights are on at The Hole in the Wall.

# November

behind barbed wire
calves huddle
staring
like children from posters
on post office walls

beyond the gates
distraught mothers mill about
bellies heaving
crying
for their abducted young

again and again they wheel
attacking the wire
the outcome
never in doubt

on command
a dog glides forward
drawing blood
on shit splattered flanks

dragged
squeezed into a truck
the young
give no answer

a handshake
the truck pulls away
labouring
under its burden

mothers search their yards
deceived by shadows
their sobs disturb the day
and trouble sleep

seven days
seven nights of grief
of chill fall wind
before they slip away

leaving tufts of hair
in the rusted wire
a reminder of a ritual
that happened last year

the year before
and will happen again
in the dark hollows of their bodies
the mothers already prepare

# relax and purr

"Lie with your eyes closed, breath deeply, and allow your body to relax. Let the others do the work and you feel the rhythm." The instructor, an earnest young man of thirty, with that mellow California look, has been lecturing for twenty minutes on massage and its effect on various parts of the human body.

Around the room a ragtag lot of people sit in a semi-circle. With the exception of my wife and three others, I have never seen any of them before. At forty-six, I am clearly the oldest, and am having the most trouble finding a comfortable position on my cushion. There isn't a chair in sight, only carpeted floor surrounded by soft pink walls. Heavy drapes conceal any sign of a window and the outside world. Soft shadows from a pottery lamp, together with the aroma of incense, casts a spell over the room, reducing voices to a whisper.

The one disruptive element, like someone appearing nude at a dress ball, involves an immense anatomy poster tacked to one wall, depicting the interior of the human body. I have studied these same posters while waiting in doctors' offices, illustrations in vivid reds and greens of dissected bowels and muscles, all the while growing ever more convinced that several of my parts must surely have malfunctioned. Today, however, I am assured by the speaker, his voice as soothing as prayer, that all is well, and if it is not, massage will soon make it so.

Across from me sits a woman who I met earlier in the week at the health food store. We had discussed the merits of different varieties of granola; she had impressed upon me the need to include pine nuts in my selection. She sits erect now, elbows on her knees, a kind of skinny Buddha, staring into space as if trying to focus on some distant planet. David, who lives across from us in our apartment block is from Singapore, here to work on a doctorate on the New Testament. He crouches now at the rear of the group, half-turned toward the door, like a rabbit about to break for cover. My wife thinks David's wife has become cool towards her since finding out they are in this group together. I hadn't noticed, but then that's the kind of thing a man can miss.

Along with the skinny Buddha and David, there is Felicity, a Roman Catholic sister with whom I am enrolled in another program on spirituality and worship. I find myself watching Felicity and trying to imagine her in a habit. Little about her resembles any sister I have known. She really isn't attractive by the usual commercial standards. But her smile is kind of naughty, like I-know-something-you-don't-but-would-you-like-to-find-out, and she has one of those marvellous earthy bodies: full breasts romping beneath a loose sweater that conceals broad hips, flat across the front. We had a teacher like her when I was in Grade 4, who would sit with her legs propped upon a chair to read to us after lunch. All the little boys strained to see what lay beyond the shadows above her knees.

I am sure I must look out of place. Born in Saskatchewan in a midwife's house, I am prairie, farm, small town, and Protestant church — church where the only reason to keep candles is fear of a power failure. After four years in a parish I grew restless; there was a whole lot about life that I needed to explore. I told everyone I was going away to study for a year in order to upgrade my skills in ministry. I didn't tell anyone, not even my wife, my real reasons for leaving and that I doubted I would ever come back.

Now I'm in Berkeley, wicked Berkeley, where on a sunny afternoon marijuana smoke drifts across the campus mingling with incense and, on occasion, tear gas. Sex is as plentiful as wine and almost as varied. I feel like a child on his first visit to the circus. Or, in the words of a friend, I have finally "runaway from home." Indeed, I am a middle-aged runaway, in the far country, that dangerous place preachers have warned about for years. The same preachers have extolled the virtues of staying home or, having left, returning as soon as possible; I have found little support for their argument.

My wife, who accompanied me on the sabbatical, is normally a more reserved person with a tendency to err on the side of caution. Keep your money in your inside pocket and obey the speed limit is her motto. So I was surprised when after dinner one evening she announced, "You know that massage class they were talking about ... I think I am going to take it."

Christ almighty, where has this come from? There is nothing strange about women taking massage classes. But, this is Berkeley and the class she is talking about consists of twenty strangers practicing massage on one another in the nude. We hadn't gone in for nudity much on the farm. Father would walk through the house balls-naked, on his way to bed after a bath. Mother had not looked kindly on such conduct and my sister had been embarrassed. On other occasions, when my parents weren't around, my cousin and I thought it quite risqué to look at women in panties in the Eaton's catalogue. Nudity, therefore, was not a thing I was accustomed to, and certainly not something in which I expected my wife to take an interest.

"Oh," I replied. "When?"

"Starts next week. Only a hundred bucks. What d'ya think?"

Word about the class had leaked out the week before. I was quite surprised to find that a number of Roman Catholic sisters in the group had taken the course in the first term. And was even more surprised to learn it was in the nude. I knew then we were in Berkeley and that there were things going on in the Roman Catholic church here that they didn't know about in Saskatchewan — and wouldn't believe if I told them. There were occasions when I found myself looking at Sister Felicity and wondering what it would be like to practice massage with her. I had even thought of various scenarios like a weekend at Carmel in a beach house or a night at the Hyatt Regency in San Francisco.

"Well, that sounds interesting. They say massage can be very enjoyable," I answer.

I have no heart for what I'm saying. In truth, I feel as if a hand has grabbed me somewhere just below my rib cage. But what can I say? Tell her not to go? Yeah, try telling the tide to go out. Tell her its fine, go and enjoy yourself, and I'll forget you are doing it. And be anxious for twelve weeks? I wander around the apartment for a time looking for the right words. Ordinarily, I would have kept my mouth shut and waited, but because of the books I have been reading, telling me of the need to be more open and sharing, I am convinced I should talk. Of course, introverts like me should never do such things. "Play your cards close to your vest and bluff the bastards," Father said. And I have been pretty good at it. One time a teacher, the same one who sat with her legs propped up, was sure I had thrown the ink that splashed on Olga, a hefty, blonde girl who sat in front of me in Grade 6. I kept my mouth shut and looked amazed. She finally blamed it on Harry, a poor devil that always looked guilty and talked too much.

"I don't know how to say this, but that massage class scares me. You won't do anything, but it bothers me."

While rehearsing the words I had thought they sounded rather good; I had been careful to include a strong "I" statement with a clear expression of my feelings. But now I felt very vulnerable. Not only that, I forgotten my wife's ability to solve such dilemmas. Confusion around such things as schedules, bank books, and lost glasses are sorted out in an instant. I could, therefore, have predicted her response.

"That's easy; come with me."

What am I to do? Stay home and be anxious, or go and be anxious? After some deliberation I decide I'm into it and can't turn back; I will do massage — in the nude.

"Well, that's about it for a start." Tension in the room rises as the instructor glances about the circle. "What I want you to do is divide into threes. One be the massagee and the other two massagers, one on the lower body, one on the upper. It works best with clothes off." As he speaks, he begins peeling off his clothes until he stands there before us in all his glory.

All of us remain seated. We start with sandals, then socks. You can take a long time getting a sock off. Pants and blouses follow. Out of the corner of my eye, I notice Felicity has indeed been blessed as generously as her sweater suggested. Underwear is given up reluctantly, folded, then stacked with care on top of the sandals. Eye contact is difficult. But where else do you look.

I can't help noticing a young, blond woman, a thin waif of a thing, no more than a girl, standing alone, forlorn, no hips, no breasts, no hair where it should have been. I want to go get my coat and drape her, protect her from eyes that should not be looking. My fatherly instincts are interrupted by a voice.

"Can I work with you and your wife?"

I turn to find Felicity and her friendly face looking up at me. "Yeah, sure, fine with me. I'll go first if you two wanna practice."

I have always had the ability to keep emotions in line when they threaten to get out of hand. Back in Grade 1 I remember going for my first vaccination. Every child in the country had gathered in the town hall where one doctor and one nurse stood waiting at a table. A hundred kids milled about at the back, like calves in a corral, waiting to be hauled off to the stockyard.

"Who's first ... somebody start." The old doctor stood there armed and ready with two syringes and two dull needles.

"I'll go," I announced, marching forward with my arm stuck out. There was a kind of gallantry in it, I suppose. First one over the top and that kind of thing. But a lot of good men are lost that way. Yet, they say at Vimy Ridge this is what made Canada a nation. But here, flat on my back, trying to breath deeply, thoughts of valour and glory never enter my mind. Survival is the objective, keeping control the goal.

My wife works on my legs while Felicity kneels behind me, my head between her knees. From here she begins to massage my face, then my neck. "Close your eyes and relax," I tell myself. I recall an incident when our daughter was three years old. She had caught our pet cat and was crouched over the animal, pressing him to the rug, saying, "Nice pussy. Relax and purr."

All seems to be going well; I have followed the rules carefully and have not opened my eyes once. My wife has worked her way down to my feet, while Felicity has done my face. Now she is bending forward to massage my upper body. My time on the floor is nearly up. I begin to imagine how I shall approach things when I am no longer the massagee. Shall I massage Felicity's top or bottom?

I cannot say for certain if I felt or heard what happened next. There is an action that lies somewhere between sound and touch for which we have no words, like petals from a plum tree blown by the wind against your lips. Such was the sensation of something, soft but firm, caressing my nose with a gentle tip tap, tip tap. My God, is this what I think it is? I can't keep the rules; I have to look. Opening my eyes ever so slightly, I look up.

King Solomon, thousands of years before, broke into song at the sight which I beheld. "Your rounded thighs are like jewels, the work of a master hand. Your navel is a rounded bowl that never lacks mixed wine. Your belly is a heap of wheat, encircled with lilies. Your breasts are like two fawns, twins of a gazelle." But Solomon, son of David, a king with wives and concubines, poet, wisdom figure, builder of the temple, ancestor of our Lord, could only stand afar describing what he saw. In Berkeley, two thousand miles from home, I heard, saw, and felt two golden fruit, clusters perfectly tapered, suspended, firm and ripe, gentle pendulums caressing my nose, tip tap, tip tap.

# better a happy house

There is a strong possibility that my wife will retire at the end of this year, a fact which causes me some anxiety. I like it here alone during the day; I can talk to myself, sleep when I please, fart with abandon. If she were to read this, I am sure she would say she fails to see how her presence has an effect on any of these activities, least of all the farting. To a point she's right, but when you put two people in a house, that is, two married folks, the situation at once demands a certain degree of order and civilized behaviour. You can rise at different times and eat breakfast when you like but once the day is up and going the joys and benefits of the marital relationship begin to kick in. Eating lunch, for example. You can't go upstairs and grab whatever is leftover; you must prepare for two. You can have a nap, but there always seems to be something happening that makes indulging in sleep almost a sin.

Or take the matter of farting. To have to hold back, which I admit doesn't happen often, or to think that someone may comment when one does get away on you, defeats the entire purpose of the exercise.

I am certain this is very much a male thing. Not that women don't break wind on occasion, but it seems to require an apology when it happens. Or a looking-about to see who in the world could have done such a thing. A few weeks back at my son's birthday party I overheard a conversation between my son and his two friends. He said that his wife had proposed a New Year's resolution for him; give up farting. Both young men shook their heads in disagreement, expressing dismay at the thought of such a thing. Of course, New Year's resolutions of any kind, but this one in particular, don't stand a chance. The entire weight of history, not to mention the requirements of the human body, are against it.

From the time I was a little boy, and I believe it was true of my friends, farting was a source of great interest and amusement. I suppose we learned it from our fathers; one could never conceive of learning such a thing from your mother. Our mothers had a powerful and lasting influence over us in many ways, but in the realm of farting fathers and uncles were our true mentors. When I mentioned this subject at breakfast with my clergy friends, one of them reported having been at a wedding reception recently where a man, during his toast to the bride, reported that he never knew that women farted until after he got married. Maybe it's one of those innate things that distinguishes the sexes; women will never fart with the gross abandon and in the varied ways common to men. Women have a totally different approach and outlook. Take my wife for instance.

A fart, especially if it happens to be of the more unpleasant variety, immediately gets her to analyzing what could possibly have caused it. Peanuts are the first culprit. Beans are next in line. I attribute it all to the parsley. The point of the exercise is to figure out the cause of the offending gas with a view to stopping it. Somehow prevention seems uppermost in a woman's mind. Norma took heart when Beano appeared on the market, a brown fluid in a little bottle that promised to relieve the build up of gastrointestinal gas throughout the world. After a year, the bottle sits on the shelf untouched. All advertising for Beano has ceased in the past few months, an unmistakable sign of another failed product.

Some feminists, I suppose, would see this discomfort with gas as one more example of injustice inflicted on women by a male dominated world. Men fart while women experience stomach discomfort and, at best, break wind hoping no one notices. I would agree with that and, by way of making some small contribution to the righting of this injustice, I say fart when ready ladies; along with careers and new found assertiveness, fart at will, and may whatever is proper be damned. It will take time, but some day equality will be achieved, although, as with pay equity, considerable effort must still be expended.

On the radio the other day a woman was interviewed about her new cookbook, one devoted entirely to the use of various kinds of beans. Of course the subject of gas arose and how it could be prevented. Soak the beans for hours. Throw the water away. Soak them again. Throw the water away. You must do this in order to rid the beans of certain chemicals which produce the action that culminates in a ... and here both host and interviewee were at a loss for words, unable to squeak out that funny little word. They giggled a little and we got the message. In defence of good cooking and beans, and farting too, I should say that when I make baked beans I do not wash and scrub the poor little buggers until all sign of their being beans has been eradicated. Boil two cups of white beans in six cups of water for two minutes. Don't throw the water away. Leave the beans soak in the same water for an hour. Simmer again for an hour and then proceed with the recipe. Imagine all the vitamins and minerals you would lose with every soaking and rinsing. Moreover, what would beans be without a little gas? And what kind of father would follow such a recipe?

Farting, like so many of our body functions and body parts, continues to be a source of humour. Our whole family laughed at my father's farting. Some of the time. Sad are the poor souls who cannot sneak a smile at an unexpected expulsion of air and the varied sounds, not to mention odour, that accompany it. There are even those more hilarious moments when there is no sound, simply odour, and only one person laughing. In fact, there remains in the English language, from sometime in the mid-1300s, a word that expresses precisely this situation: fizzle — as in fizzle out — meaning to break wind without noise. All of which reminds me of a few years back when I decided to deepen my prayer life.

My yearly physical revealed I had high blood pressure. Among the various remedies suggested was transcendental meditation. Knowing little about it, I signed up and paid my money. To my surprise the "courses" consisted of watching a video, along with seven other people, for two hours once a week for eight weeks. Even more surprising was the content: the Indian guru, Marharashi Yogi, sat on a carpet twirling a rose, promising in a squeaky voice to cure everything from poverty to war by getting a few more people to meditate twenty minutes a day. Somewhere in there he would fix my high blood pressure.

One evening as he droned on about world peace and love, someone fizzled — no sound, just the fumes, one of the most foul odours I have ever encountered, human or otherwise. Kids would fizzle in school and everyone would look around trying to identify the culprit. We would blame it on the guy who was laughing. Sometimes a particular smell was associated with a certain kid. Among the eight mediators, however, it was impossible to tell who had fizzled; everyone continued serenely in the midst of the fumes. After a moment or two the gas lifted, but then it happened again. And again. For that entire evening, at regular intervals, someone in our midst would lay down another. And since I didn't do it and I was the only male present, it had to be a woman. No one had the nerve to get up and leave. Or risk making an accusation. To have said anything without proof might simply have caused the finger of suspicion to point at the accuser and not the offender. I survived the evening and even learned a little about meditating, although war, poverty, and my blood pressure have remained at about the same level. The lasting effect has been the laughter that erupts each time I remember that little man in his saffron robe twirling a rose, promising peace, when all I could think of was drawing my next breath.

In researching this topic I looked on the Internet. If you can believe it, when I punched in "farting" there came up 5,250 matches covering every aspect of the subject one could imagine. Somehow such a volume of material, like so much of what appears on the Internet, an amassing of more and more information without any distinction as to quality, dampened my interest. Like reading that sign at McDonald's, "Billions and billions served," and trying to find some pleasure in eating a hamburger. Deflated me, I suppose you could say. I downloaded nothing and closed the screen, choosing instead to rely on sources that treat the subject with a little more dignity.

I contacted a few select friends who I thought would know something of the subject, if not from an academic point of view, then certainly from experience. A gentleman, with a doctorate to his name and a distinguished career in the academic world to his credit, was somewhat reluctant to speak for fear I would quote him saying, "An old fart who lives on my street said ..."; I assured him I would not make his name public. He put me in touch with The Oxford English Dictionary and the Oxford Dictionary of Slang. I contacted two professors of English at the University of Saskatchewan who assured me that farting had a long history in English literature and suggested I look into the works of Chaucer and Alexander Pope.

I discovered that the use of the word *fart*, along with several other terms related to the human body, was common in the English language throughout the Middle Ages. Somewhere along the way such words slipped into disrepute. Fizzled out. As a result, modern editors invariably associate fart with vulgar language, straining to express themselves with terms such as gastrointestinal gas and flatulence — a bit of high pitched wind when a good fart would have said it all. Earlier writers were not so restricted.

Samuel Johnson writing in the mid-1700s, and still considered one of England's better writers and literary critics, produced, among other things, a massive work known as the *Dictionary of The English Language*. When he comes to the word fart he doesn't bother to give a learned definition such as "an emission of gas blah, blah, blah." Rather he offers two poems, the first from another noted English writer Jonathan Swift:

> As when we a gun discharge
> Although the bore be ne'er so large
> Before the flame from muzzle burst
> Just as at the breach it flashes first
> So from my lord his passion broke
> He farted first and then he spoke.

The second poem he wrote himself:

> Love is the fart
> of every heart
> It pains a man when 'tis kept clofe
> And others doth offend, when 'tis let loofe.

And then there's Chaucer, a learned man, the first to give the English language prestige as a means of communicating the best that could be thought or said. And who wrote of farting as naturally as the act itself in his most famous work *The Canterbury Tales*. Reading in the old English is near impossible, at least I haven't the time or energy, but fortunately we now have prose versions in modern English, more readable even if they lose something in translation.

Chaucer has one of the pilgrims, the miller, who told a story about an elderly carpenter and his beautiful young wife. Of course, a younger man, in this case two younger men — Nicholas and Absolon — become more than a little interested in her. The wife is quite attracted to Nicholas, and encourages their meeting, but will have nothing to do with Absolon. In a bizarre turn of events, she is in bed with Nicholas when the unwanted Absolon comes courting, singing to her outside her bedroom window. In the dark, she tells Absolon he can have one kiss and sticks her arse out the window, which he kisses. "A beard, a beard," cries Absolon and then he realizes she has made a fool of him. Cured of his obsession, he sets out for revenge. He gets a hot plough shear from the blacksmith and returns, still singing his love song and asking for another kiss. Only this time Nicholas decides to get in on the act and puts his arse out the window. Then Nicholas let off a great fart like a thunderclap. Absolon, almost blinded with the blast, had his hot iron ready and smote Nicholas plumb on the bum.

I suppose there is always the chance I could be suffering from some perversion but I find delight in that story. It would be an insult to say, as we do of the usual sex story, that it's funny. There is something humorous about it being so ordinary, where farting is such a natural thing. It is the same delight I have encountered each time I have raised the issue whether it be with clergy, professors, or the next door neighbour. A number of women have contributed. There have been numerous phone calls and one email offering information, often a personal story of farting in the family or on the part of one's spouse. Invariably laughter erupts.

96

At home on the farm we had a stairwell leading to the upstairs. I don't know if Father planned it or not, but as he was retiring for the evening, near the top of the stairs there would come this blast that would echo between the walls and then seem to roll down into the living room. We became more or less accustomed to it with no more than an occasional comment from my mother like, "I hope that man is all right." I told this story on the phone the other night to a friend, an Anglican priest, and he at once began laughing. His father had done the same thing, except his eruptions had come early in the morning. Beyond the health benefits involved, it acted as a sort of alarm clock, his father booming away and his mother uttering her husband's name in mild disgust at 7 a.m. every morning.

I am sure Norma's retirement will go well. There is a saying that originated somewhere in Ontario, a way of saying excuse me when you really are quite pleased with what you have done: better a happy house than an angry tenant. I had forgotten the exact wording, but she remembered.

# of saints and other things

It was early morning at writer's school, and before me stretched a long day of working with words: reading, writing, sitting in a group trying to appear informed. I had come to the game late; there were people in the group younger than my children, with manuscripts near completion and whose knowledge of writing would be forever beyond me. I felt intimidated, uptight. Then, suddenly, it was as if my father were standing there.

"Tight as a bull's arse," he said, a look of glee on his face, an expression that signalled a kind of devil be damned confidence, even when reality indicated otherwise.

Probably the saying originated with an old uncle or with somebody he heard in the streets of Quebec where he grew up. Where it came from before that no one will ever know. It has the sound of Ireland to it. Whatever the case, while originally not meant to apply to one's emotional state, but more to objects binding against one other, in my depressed and fearful condition the words had a strange appeal. Suddenly I found myself lying on my bed laughing.

"Tight as a bull's arse in fly time" was what Father really said; he rarely said ass, always arse. "You need that like a dog needs two arse holes" was a way of saying I didn't need whatever it was I wanted. While I may have disagreed with his assessment of my need, the image and its meaning were perfectly clear. Or he would say, "Put your arse into it, my boy," not a command, but a kind of urging on, a coach's plea for a little more effort. Nothing negative about it, just a clear image of what was required. At other times, such as when a fight broke out between my sister and I, he would observe, "Me arse and the fight was on." Such a phrase defies explanation except that it conveys perfectly the nature of fights that break out between siblings or between neighbours who have had an ongoing feud for years. Like the statement, there is an eruptive quality to such battles, fights which generally have little at stake, possessed of more noise than substance and which, above all, serve as a source of amusement for those watching from the sidelines. Me arse and the fight was on; I suppose you could say it was a kind of cheer that went up from my father as he watched from a distance.

Ass. Arse. Ass sounds unfriendly. Hostile. Stupid ass. Her ass is two axe handles wide, descriptive though it may be, it has an unpleasant, vulgar connotation, a characteristic which I associate with American profanity. But an arse two axe handles wide has something suggestive about it, earthy, breadth and depth, a poetic ring suggesting infinite possibilities. More civilized, more English. A humour to it, like the old sergeant saying, "If those are wild oats, my arse is a blow torch."

I was part of an army summer training program. On this particular day we were out running around learning how to kill people, if the need should ever arise, and had stopped for dinner near an abandoned farm. In the field stood a few stocks of grain, which one of the cadets identified as wild oats. Enter sergeant with his comments about his arse and the blow torch. An argument followed as to who was right.

"Ask Evans; he lived on a farm."

"Evans. What's this plant?" roared the sergeant.

I came running over from my shaded spot under a tree and took a look.

"Wild oats, Sergeant."

A chorus of voices went up: "Look out, Sergeant's arse is a blow torch."

There have been many occasions similar to that morning at writer's school when I have felt intimidated and stupid, times which, when I reflect on it, have been invariably associated with school.

Grade 3. I had an average of 93, but my cousin had an average of 93.7 and I felt like I had failed. Later, in high school math and science, subjects at which my mother excelled and could not understand why I did not, were a continual struggle. I thought for quite some time that I was stupid, and even yet, under the right conditions, the old scripts return. Probably the worst case of feeling stupid occurred when I returned to graduate school at the age of twenty-eight.

Initially in our family, Grade 12 and a Bachelor of Arts held sufficient prestige and promise. Off in the distance, spoken of with awe, was the possibility of a doctorate, a status reserved for the special few, the really smart ones. A doctorate could be dreamed of, suggested. A master's degree would be acceptable, although I had the feeling it was something like getting 93 instead of 94. At any rate, I would settle for going to graduate school and a master's, one rung from the top. But even this was quite enough for the stupid jitters to set in.

Along with the aura of graduate school there were other factors adding to the pressure. I was in Berkeley, California, a place which, in the minds of most Saskatchewan people in 1965 suggested warmth, oranges, and ocean, San Francisco and Los Angeles; the Golden Gate Bridge and movie stars. But I was sure I had dust in my ears and cow shit on my shoes, all of which were surely noticeable to those around me. Years later, I understood what culture shock meant. But it was the classroom itself that was most troubling: new ideas, students who I assumed were smarter than I, massive amounts of reading. I was running to catch up and I felt stupid, little realizing, of course, that there were many others who felt the same way. In graduate school you don't mention such things.

In the midst of this stupid spell, a character appeared who was to contribute significantly to my salvation: Martin Luther of Protestant Reformation fame.

I remember the day in the library, feeling like I had been thrown in at the deep end, coming upon Luther's *Table Talk*, a volume of material consisting not of Luther's well-reasoned theology, but rather a collection of his "spur of the moment" comments and ideas, copied down by a friend while Luther conversed over a meal or mug of beer — perhaps several. "Anyone who would write a book," said Luther, "should first smell the fart of an old sow." At once I felt the burden of graduate school begin to lift; someone had been here before me and had had the courage to speak. There were many other comments in a similar vein — rough and vulgar, but expressive of a piece of the truth I felt I had lost.

I read a lot of Luther that fall, in time appreciating the awe and wonder that fell over him when he realized that his own efforts to save himself were of no avail; the resolution of his struggle lay elsewhere. But it was his comments about the old sow and books that first caught my attention and helped turn me in another direction. An old sow, a fart, and a book: a means of grace.

It strikes me now that figures like Luther and my father are saints even though Protestants don't believe in such things. We threw saints out with a whole lot of other things that we might well have kept. I believe in saints, characters like Luther and my father who happened along at the right time with a word that saved.

Arse, then, is essential. A bull's arse in fly time. How tight can a nut be on a bolt? Or a cutting knife wedged in the guards of a mower? How intimidated can you be at writer's school, feeling like you are too old and too late?

# remembering the queen's toilet

in seventeen hundred b.c.e
on the island of Crete
the queen at Knossus
had a flush toilet
in a city without walls
or implements of war
artists painted eyeshadowed women
and scenes of young men leaping
horned bulls extraordinaire

three thousand five hundred
years before the Anglicans
ordained a woman
three thousand five hundred
years before T. Crapper
created England's first
shall we say commode
three thousand two hundred
years before the pope
draped Rome's nudes
Minoans blessed priestesses
with soft bare nippled breasts
while on sun drenched walls and temple pillars

muscled bulls
wore their organs proudly
and Minoans
without benefit of clergy
or a department of defence
knew the art of love

# the only subject

Baptism and a death sentence. To be more precise my grandson's baptism and Salman Rushdie's death sentence.

Over a year ago I baptized my grandson, an event over which I felt no small amount of ambivalence. Only now have I stopped to reflect on what I did and have found unexpected assistance from Salman Rushdie who has lived for ten years under the sentence of death.

I would have been disappointed if I had not been asked to baptize my grandson. At the same time I had misgivings. Clergy who make a practice of marrying and burying relatives and being the man of prayer for the family have always been a little suspect in my eyes. The role never appealed to me. Of course, I have gone to the other extreme: I have had one wedding and one baptism involving family in almost forty years. The baptism was of my mother-in-law and I couldn't very well refuse. As for my niece's wedding, I began to see a problem in that she had five sisters. If they all asked me to marry them and they all had an average of three children, that adds up to a lot of weddings and baptisms — or baptisms and weddings, as sometimes happens. Even if several chose, as has been the case, to proceed "without benefit of clergy," the numbers would still have been high. Flimsy excuses, I know, but these were the ones I gave. With my grandson there were other problems, at least in my mind, of a more immediate nature.

The first obstacle was where to meet; I don't have a church. Then do it at home. In the park. No. There is a dignity involved, a presence that a church provides. The town hall or my living room will not do. I spoke with a friend, a minister in a local church and he said, "Do the baptism here in our chapel. We will set it all up. Just name a date and clear it with the secretary." One hurdle cleared.

But baptism is done as part of a community, part of a church body. What would we do for people? Baptism is more than water and a few words by a doting grandfather. There must be people. And words. What words would we use? Do you reject Satan, father of sin and prince of darkness? Do you believe in God the Father Almighty, maker of heaven and earth ... ? Heavy stuff. As symbol and poetry I love that language, but I don't "believe" it. How will my children hear it? And what would I say if they asked me what I believed? They didn't ask. A date was set and the chapel reserved.

At about this time I stopped for breakfast with a Mennonite clergy friend. I should say I have had a kind of love/hate relationship with the Mennonites, an attitude originating far back in the shadows of family. Generations ago my mother's people were Pennsylvania Dutch, kissing cousins to the Mennonites, belonging to a church known as The Plymouth Brethren, some of whom migrated from Lancaster county in Pennsylvania to Eastern Canada. By the time my mother's family reached Saskatchewan, their religious life had deteriorated to involvement in a dark little sect known as the Gospel Hall, which, as near as I can tell, kept most of what was evil about religion and discarded the good. In Saskatoon the church split over whether or not to have an organ in the church.

Fortunately, Mother jettisoned much of the nonsense associated with the group, but the early years left a mark. My family may have been far removed from buggies and beards, but the crippled ghosts of that old religion remained. There were distinctions between right and wrong without much room between, a lingering suspicion of anything pleasurable and an embarrassment with things sexual. There are times when I hear those old ghosts and they make me nervous. Sometimes they take over the house. Mennonites remind me of all this history, but I also admire them. One finds a sense of community in their midst and a stubborn will to do what they believe is good, not just because it is a nice thing to do, but rather because they have been commanded to serve.

Anyway, I told my friend about my dilemma. I was going to baptize my grandson, and with only a week left I didn't know what I was doing, or why. Nor did I know what I was going to say.

"I think that's wonderful that they would ask you to do the baptism. As far as what they believe, I wouldn't let it get in the way. You know, I would guess that well over half the young people I meet with are in just that same position. There is a residue of faith that remains and they respond from that. So I see it as one way to be with them, to say something which I hope will let them know that God loves them and their child. I think that's what the church is about."

Over half the people are in the same position. A residue of faith. The words kept echoing throughout the day. I wrote them down that evening along with a few other notes, intending to come back to them when I had time.


Norma and I arrived at the church early. While she set up the coffee and arranged some flowers, I rehearsed what I was going to do, candles, readings — what I was going to say.

I had hoped all our family would come, including my daughter Suzanne, but she informed us the day before that friends had arrived from Ottawa and she was caught up entertaining them; they might go canoeing. I suspected she had other reasons, but, although disappointed, I decided there was nothing I could do and settled for her not being there. Then, to my surprise, she and the boating party appeared, in all states of dress: rubber boots, cut-offs, back packs, etc. I invited them all to stay and they gladly accepted. By two o'clock everyone had arrived: parents and child, maternal grandparents, and two sisters with their families. Two of our neighbours whom we had invited were also present. One sister and her husband had agreed to be godparents. The chairs were set up in a half-circle for about a dozen people. The canoe party had taken seats behind the circle, but we added more chairs and there we all were, a dress or two, rubber boots, and me in a suit. Several children ran in and out.

Wrapped in a knitted shawl, Jackson Alexander Evans slept. His
parents had given him the name without remembering that my father's
name was John Alexander Evans or was more commonly known as J.A.
Evans. I saw that name often on cheques, in the paper, in minute
books. Now I was to baptize Jackson Alexander Evans, who some day
might have his own bank account and sign his name J.A. Evans.

We lit the candles. I read from Psalm 84: "How lovely is thy
dwelling place/O lord of hosts/My heart longs, yea, faints/for the courts
of the lord ... Even the sparrow finds a home/and the swallow a nest for
herself." Suzanne read from the Gospel of Mark about the children and
mothers who Jesus called back after they had been sent away by the dis-
ciples. It was one of my mother's favourite stories.

Then I said a few words about what I thought baptism was about. It
was the commitment of the parents, the family, and church. But finally
it was an event in which we did not know what we were doing. I didn't
tell them of my misgivings of the previous days and that I was indeed
speaking for myself. Baptism is something that God is about and in
which we are participants. As I spoke I found myself missing a word, losing track of what I had prepared, but going on with what I wanted to say.
I was nervous and making mistakes, but I knew it really didn't matter.

I asked the questions of belief and commitment of the mother and
father, the godparents, and the people, and they all answered. Then we
came to the baptism and time for me to take Jackson. This will sound
rather strange, but in the baptisms I had done previously, I had never
held the child, leaving him or her in the arms of the parents. There
were various reasons for this. Partly, I had no models. Baptism was
never discussed or worked through in seminary in any way other than
a few lectures, by reading some books, and writing a sterile essay. Nor
had I seen many baptisms in church. It was never a high priority, a
reflection of the theological malaise of the United Church of Canada.
More than this, however, I was just not comfortable taking the child.
It seemed so much easier to leave a child be and cause as little distur-
bance as possible. At least that's the reasons I gave. But I was determined to change all this, at least for an afternoon.

I took Jackson from his mother and was pleased at the way he fit
neatly in the crook of my arm. "I baptize you in the name of the Father

... of the Son ... and the Holy Spirit." Only when the water began to run down over his head did he stretch and waken for a moment, then return to sleep. We went for a walk around the circle and everyone had a chance to talk and look. Jackson slept on. I had wanted the baptism to go well, but it was only as I stood in the middle of the circle looking at the child that I realized, for reasons I did not understand nor had I planned for, how beautiful a moment it was.

We closed with prayers and a blessing, and then stopped for coffee and cake while the children ran free.

It was in this state of looking back that I came upon a comment by Salman Rushdie. He reflects on what has happened to him since receiving news on February 14, 1989, of his being placed on a hit list by Iranian authorities because they viewed the book *Satanic Verses* as blasphemous.

The years have been difficult for Rushdie, not to mention dangerous. Yet, he says he has grown; not only has his writing improved, most importantly he has rededicated himself, "determined to prove that the high art of writing is more resilient than what menaces it." But that wasn't what first caught my attention; rather it was his reflections concerning Valentine's Day, a day of love on which he received a notice of death. Rushdie writes: "... these dark anniversaries of the appalling valentine I was sent in 1989 have also been times to reflect upon the countervailing value of love. Love feels more and more like the only subject. At the centre of my life, of my new work, of my future plans, I now find nothing else."

Baptizing one's grandson would seem to be a long way from being under a death sentence for ten years, but there are similarities. How do you explain a baptism or a death sentence? Oh yes, I know all the reasons, but from a reasoned point of view neither a baptism nor a death sentence make any sense. Then there is the matter of control. When you're baptized, much like being shot, you have it done to you. You receive. Neither of the participants, Jackson or Salman Rushdie, could do a thing except receive what was done to them. That's the nature of baptizing people and planning their death; the matter is out of the recipient's hands.

One other similarity: both acts, a baptism and the threat of death, have unexpected results. You just don't know how things will turn out.

I don't know what Jackson took away from the baptism or what will be the outcome for him; we will know something of that in time. Nor do I know what the baptism meant for others, but, unexpectedly, with my own "residue of faith" I know a little of what I received. More than that, I appreciate Rushdie when he says, for all that has occurred in the past, as unreasonable as events have been and as helpless as he was in the face of them, love feels more and more like the only subject.

# a love story

There were other bachelors in the country: George, a shy man who may well have longed for a partner other than a wife, Bob, the Scotsman who pulled his own tooth with a pair of pliers; and Old Mac, Albert McNaughton, whose shack finally burned to the ground when the ashes from the stove accumulated and burned through the floor. Bereft of his shack, he went mad and died in a mental hospital.

But it was Carl I admired, and whose shack I enjoyed the most. I was simply a bystander, a boy sitting on a chair listening, while he and my father talked about farming, politics, and gossip. You learned who was in trouble with the police, who was pregnant and shouldn't be, priceless information that made one an authority at school the next day. Bachelors seemed to know about such things.

Carl had been born of old German stock in Minnesota in a town named Zumbrota. He and his friend Barney had taken to the road sometime before 1920, "riding the rails," young men in search of adventure. Carl told how the two of them, in order to get off a train without being caught by the police, would wait until the freight slowed near a town, then take a running leap from their boxcar and roll down the cinder littered embankment. The worst that ever resulted was a few bruises and scrapes. They drifted north into Canada where they found work driving horses on a construction project in Alberta. On one occasion a foreman ordered Barney to do something which Barney thought endangered the horses. He refused and was fired. Such was their relationship that Carl quit on the spot and they moved on.

In time the two men parted company, and Carl, like a ball of Russian thistle blown before the wind, came to rest in Saskatchewan, snagged by a quarter section of land and the friendship of one or two farmers. He built a house which, as was the case with bachelor dwellings regardless of size or looks, was always referred to as "the shack." Only one thing could elevate a shack to the status of house: marriage and the presence of a wife. It was something Carl would strive for throughout much of his life, but never achieve.

You entered Carl's shack via the porch, a lean-to which served as a general catch-all for tools, spare clothes, machine parts, and whatever else happened to be in season. Junk had collected until only a narrow passage remained — a path worn through the floor boards to the earth beneath.

Beyond the porch lay the main room where, if you stood in the middle, you could reach everything you needed without moving more than a step. To one side stood the stove, an old flat top with a black pipe extending through the ceiling. The place should have burned to the ground, but never did. Sitting on the stove were the two essentials in a bachelor's kitchen: a coffee pot and a frying pan. Invariably the coffee was a day old and the grease in the pan a quarter-inch deep, a leftover from the last meal and several meals before that. Good bachelors knew that soap and water ruined a frying pan. On a nail by the wash basin hung a towel that had wiped off more dirt than water. A table, three chairs, and a bed in the corner rounded out the furniture, everything, almost, that a man required.

Some bachelors were a little "rough around the edges," but others like Carl dressed well, owned a car, and had a dollar to spend. Of some it was said, "They would make a good catch." Once in awhile it would happen; one did get caught. Or ran fast enough to catch up. Easily overlooked in this discussion is the status, or should I say, the plight of women.

My father holding his grandson with my father's close friend Carl Weckerling.

There were those women who made the decision to remain single, unwilling to take up residence in the countryside and endure the life that lay in store for them. If this was their choice, however, it consigned them to the unappealing category of spinster or, worse yet, old maid. Spinster suggested a devoted soul, head down, spinning her wheels. Old maid carried an even deeper insult. What name did we give to the burned kernels of corn that failed to pop? It would have been unthinkable for a woman to live alone or to have a shack. And to "shack up" was an act akin to acquiring leprosy. Women had a choice: marry, become a nun, or end up a burned kernel rattling about in the bottom of the pot.

As for Carl, he remained in the bachelor category, although this was always in doubt. On Saturday night he became something of a knight errant, a Don Quixote in search of his own Dulcinea. But reality always overcame him. Over the years he left in his wake a trail of failed love affairs, all of them in their own way doomed from the beginning. I heard of three such relationships and witnessed his heartbreak at the break-up of a fourth.

Carl had been drinking heavily when he arrived at our home on a Sunday afternoon in July. His girlfriend, a woman much younger, had

113

taken up with another man. It was natural that he should turn to my parents for support, especially my father. In the early days of settlement when my father had arrived from Quebec, eighteen years old and ill prepared for the ways of farming, it was Carl he turned to for direction. Carl became something of a mentor and a bond grew between the men. In later years the relationship shifted somewhat, Carl increasingly relying on my father for advice and support in a changing world, affairs of the heart no exception.

After pouring out his grief, Carl drove away, alone in his half-ton truck. Later I rescued his upper dentures from the dog who had found the teeth on the ground, where Carl, for reasons only a drunk and broken hearted man can understand, had lost them.

Just this year, some thirty-five years after Carl's death, I learned details of an earlier and, it would appear, a more involved relationship.

A woman of the community had been left alone after her husband, for reasons unknown, returned to his home in the U.S. To survive she moved to a small house near Carl's. Here she "took in his washing," a euphemism which appears to have covered a variety of activities. After a time, she suddenly moved away to British Columbia. Here a son was born.

Had the relationship developed sixty years later, the couple would have lived together, borne a son and raised a family. A young woman would have had a home and perhaps not have moved across the country. "The shack" would have been a house with children. But again, the girl who got pregnant, the woman who messed around, had few options.

One other detail: the son returned to Saskatchewan as a young man where he stopped to visit with this bachelor who bore his name. From all reports, the boy had done well. His name was Carl.

Is it too much to hope that one old bachelor, even though he couldn't share it, took pride in a son and in being a father? And somewhere a mother forgave herself and took satisfaction in having done her best? Surely they remembered evenings when the shack was transformed, a place where, for a few nights, one room with a ramshackle lean-to became a home.

# every so often I need reminding

*a girl*

I say girl because when I first saw her she looked young, no more than
a child. She had given birth to an infant with deformities so severe it
was certain the baby could live no more than a few hours. Baptism was
requested. When I arrived at Intensive Care, the girl's mother was present, but there was no sign of other family. After a time the young mother was brought from her room and stood there, wide eyed, looking like
a fawn flushed from hiding. I was grateful for the nurse, in her early
twenties herself, who took the girl by the arm and brought her close to
the incubator. It was all the girl could do to look at the tubes and needles, and distorted bit of flesh. "It's all right," the nurse assured her,
reaching through the opening and stroking a tiny hand. "You can touch
him if you like." The girl stepped closer, shaking, and for a moment held
the hand of her child, then stepped back and the baptism proceeded.

An hour later, I received another call. The child had died and the
family wanted to have a memorial service in the chapel. Arrangements
were made for the afternoon. When the hour arrived three more people were present, among them a youth who appeared as uncomfortable
and frightened as the young mother had. I wondered what I should do.

"You can touch him if you like." It was the voice of the young
woman. How different she looked; clearly a transformation had
occurred. She stepped to the side of the bassinet and turned back the

blanket, then took the young man's hand. Together they stroked the face of their son.

*a young man*

His name was Ivan, a young aboriginal man picked up at two in the morning trying to steal a truck. All he succeeded in doing was smashing up the interior of the vehicle. It was more an act of violence than theft. Three thousand dollars damage and a six week jail sentence resulted, not to mention the frustration and anger that was generated in all those who were affected. The estimate was that Ivan would be in jail for three weeks. Obviously, he was released sooner; I read about him two weeks later in the paper. The headline said something to the effect that a man had been beaten and was near death. Two men had been arrested and charged with assault. One of them was Ivan. The paper reported that the victim died, and Ivan would be charged with murder. A week later, he received a sentence of life in prison.

I never met Ivan. I only heard of him and the havoc he created over a period of weeks. It is not difficult to imagine what his life was like before these events and we know what life will be like for him for several years to come. In the grip of rage and hate, it is hard to imagine life ever being different.

*an old woman*

She was sitting alone in the waiting room when I first saw her, perhaps eighty years of age, plain looking with sunburned face and arms — probably from a small town or farm. Yet, here in this strange environment she carried herself with a look of confidence and dignity. She told me her son had been injured in a car accident and she was waiting. In a few minutes a doctor arrived. "I'm sorry," he said. "We did all we could, but we couldn't save him. Too much damage to his brain. I'm sorry." He stood uncomfortably for a moment and then turned away.

She looked away for a time, staring into space, but did not weep. A nurse approached with papers to sign.

"I want to see my son." The woman's voice was clear and firm, her words as much a command as a request.

"No, that will not be possible; he has been taken to the morgue."

"I want to see him."

"But that would be difficult."

"I will wait."

"But he was hurt badly and has not been prepared."

"That doesn't matter; I want to see my son."

"Are you sure?"

"Yes."

Unable to dissuade her, the head nurse and I escorted the woman to the morgue. I waited with the woman in the hall while the nurse went inside and made what preparations she could for viewing the body.

Morgues are not the most comforting of places: stainless steel slabs, gurneys, green sheets, temperature near freezing. But the old woman didn't seem to notice nor was she troubled by the gravel that had been ground into one side of her son's face. "Yes, that's him," she said. We stepped aside while she stood at the gurney for several minutes, talking softly. Then she turned, hugged both of us, and thanked us for what we had done.

*a mother*

I got a call from a woman whose eleven-year-old daughter had died a month before from leukemia; she was grieving and her family wanted her to talk to someone. Could she talk to me? I agreed to meet her the next day. When I make appointments like this I find myself trying to visualize who will appear. My impression, a stereotype I suppose, is that people seeking counselling tend to have more of most things — education, income, expectations and, above all, hang-ups, real or imagined. Life was supposed to go well, it isn't, and I can fix it.

The woman who appeared at my door the next day was wearing jeans and was on the edge of being overweight. She had a matter-of-fact confidence about her, a what-you-see-is-what-you-get look, and began telling me at once what had happened.

"My daughter was diagnosed with cancer last year. The doctor said it was a bad kind but they would try to stop it. I said to her, 'Promise me that you will fight and beat this thing. Never give up.' She agreed and for eight months she did fight. We had chemo, a bone marrow transplant — the works. It went into remission, I guess you call it, and for a little while we thought maybe we had made it. But then it came back, full blown. The doctor gave her two weeks.

One night it was awful. She was in pain — couldn't get comfortable. I was holding her and she began telling me, 'Mom, you have been a good mother and you have done everything you could.' She went on like this for awhile and then I understood. I said to her, 'You know that promise you made to me ... you don't have to keep it. If you have to go you can go.' She went to sleep in my arms and died two days later."

I sat there with tears in my eyes. Beautiful, beautiful was all I could say. The woman looked at me surprised and said she didn't understand. I told her it was one of the most beautiful stories I had ever heard, painful yes, but beautiful.

I remember these stories, the words, the faces, as clearly as if they had happened yesterday. I can be depressed or afraid, bitching or plodding along putting one foot in front of the other. Then I see the girl who became a woman in three hours, or Ivan who could only hate. I hear a mother telling her daughter she doesn't have to keep her promise.

All at once it's like one of those prairie mornings that comes in February. Fresh snow. One rabbit track across the white. Bitter cold and you can see for miles.

# of poppy seed and cabbage rolls

A woman to the north of our farm, a Serbian immigrant and an excellent cook, for some special occasion made a poppy seed cake and gave it to my parents. Today poppy seed cake rates as a fine dessert but, because my parents had never heard of such food, they threw the cake out. Not only was it peculiar food, it had been made by a "Ukrainian." She and thousands of other immigrants like her, had arrived in western Canada from eastern Europe following WW I. To the population already present, of which my family was a part, these newcomers were simply "the Ukrainians" and as such were looked upon with an attitude, if not of contempt, certainly of superiority.

Of course, we had good reason for such an outlook; we were English.


The three men, one Scottish, one English, and the other Irish, had all served England in one or the other of her various wars. Andy had been a member of the Scotch Grays, a proud regiment that rode only grey horses, and had fought in the Boer war and later in WW I. "The majah" had served in "Indjha" and, by way of proof, had a huge white moustache appropriate to a major's rank and wore a pith helmet, the very one he had worn to the officers' mess, if not in battle. Fred, it was assumed, fought in WW I. When drunk, which was often, Fred and Andy re-fought various battles in which they were supposed to have participated. It was noted that Fred, in keeping with the Irish tendency to embellish a story, invariably had three hundred thousand troops while Andy had only a hundred.

In truth, these men, and many more like them, represented the debris of the British colonial system. They had been encouraged by the Canadian government to come to Canada to settle the west; while at the same time they were urged on by an English government, only too glad to be rid of them, people for whom it no longer had a war to fight, but felt some obligation to support.

This is not to say they were not good people; just misplaced. Fred was a great storyteller, known especially for his figures of speech, many of which I memorized as a child, aphorisms like "Blacker than the Earl of Hell's riding boot" or "So damn far away it'll take five dollars to send a penny post card." I remember five verses of a naughty little ditty Fred sang when he was high, sung to the tune of "The Wearin' of the Green." Fred's wife was a nurse, the only source of medical advice available for miles. You went to her with your aches and pains but mostly for an ear that listened. Andy was a loyal and trusted friend. His wife, Maggie, was the babysitter who put massive amounts of butter, brown sugar, and cinnamon on my toast. The "majha", although an arrogant man, remained a symbol of the English spirit, a reminder in tough times that although the situation might be hopeless it was not serious.

Having said this, however, the fact remains that these men couldn't farm, couldn't learn to farm, and should never have been near a farm. Apart from their lack of skill and aptitude for agriculture, their greatest handicap was a sense of privilege arising out of an ingrained belief in the myth of king and empire, in short, an unquestioned confidence that the finer things of life could only be English in origin.

While difficult to admit, this was the attitude that prevailed, and my family and I were part of it. We too were "English," a general term that included all those who had arrived around the turn of the century in the first layer of immigration, people from Ontario, the British Isles, and the U.S. We had gained a toehold in the land, had a good education for the day, and knew the language. Discrimination? Or was it racism? Whatever the case it's embarrassing to remember that we called the poppy seed cake maker a "bohunk." Even our indiscriminate use of the term "Ukrainian" was an insult in that we used it to refer to anyone remotely connected to Eastern Europe: Poles, Russians, Hungarians, Serbs, Croats. This, of course, overlooks the fact that we had not distinguished that there were people who originated in the Ukraine and were Ukrainian. What did it matter? They all had an accent that sounded somewhat the same, liked garlic, made homebrew, and ate peculiar food. They were different and did things so un-English.

"They'll have half of the first nickel they ever made."

My father's words refer to Peter and Mike, two Serbs who worked for him in the 1920s picking stones from a quarter section of prairie in preparation for breaking. Stories of their work habits and thrift were still told in my time, accounts of how they would sort through the manure pile, a place on the far side of a hill beyond the barn where we dumped manure and garbage of all kinds. They would retrieve worn out rubber boots, cut them down, and wear the bottoms as shoes, holding their new found footwear in place with rubber sealer rings. Strips of gunny sack wrapped about their feet served as socks. After a day of picking stones, the toughest job one could find on a farm, they would snare gophers for which they received a penny a tail from the municipality, two cents if it was a good year. They had reason to work in such a fashion; back in their homeland wives and children waited for passage money for the trip to Canada.

Most of these new immigrants were far better equipped to wrestle with the weather and the land of Western Canada than were Andy, Fred and "the Majah." Many had been farmers in the land they had left behind, accustomed to hard work and making a living with their hands. Political and economic conditions had toughened these people in other ways, preparing them for what lay ahead. In time, as difficult as the land and the English could be, the Peters and Mikes and the women that followed after them, were to become prosperous farmers, business people, and artists.

The discrimination that occurred is difficult to admit now, embarrassing. But this is not the whole of the story or where the story can be allowed to end.

1918. When my mother arrived at her first school at the age of seventeen, it was in an area initially settled by farmers who had come from
Ontario and the United States. Now it was filling with new immigrants
from all parts of Europe. One of the immediate problems that arose was
an outbreak of head lice, brought into the school by some of the newly
arrived children. My mother was familiar with head lice having experienced them as a child in the move to western Canada. The cure was
a treatment of coal oil and water, followed by a good scrubbing. All this
she did with her students and the head lice were cleared up, only to
appear again a few days later. But now some of the parents arrived asking how she had cured the problem. She showed them how and the
head lice were gone for good. Between her and the people there developed a deep sense of respect. Years later I would meet some of these
same people, all of whom spoke of my mother with affection.

A similar relationship developed around my father, although for
different reasons.

A car appears in the yard from which emerges a grizzled old farmer in
overalls. Father approaches and they shake hands. Such scenes are a
common occurrence. As reeve of the municipality people are continu-
ally coming to him, especially the new immigrants, seeking assistance
in stickhandling the system.

Before the visitor gets down to business, however, a ritual unfolds.
He produces a bottle and both men have a drink, but in a manner not
quite in keeping with proper English etiquette. Rather than offering
Father a drink, the visitor first takes a drink himself and then passes the
bottle. In time, we came to understand that rather than being discour-
teous, taking a drink first was an act of concern and friendship after the
fashion of medieval kings who had servants taste their food before they
ate, lest it be poisoned. When the drink was homebrew such courtesy
was no small matter.

An abiding sense of trust and respect developed between my father
and these newcomers with strange ways. He told of being invited to
weddings, joyous occasions that could go on for two and three days.
Old Croatian men hugged him, planting great wet kisses on his cheek,

an expression of affection to which he was not accustomed. For his part he treated these men and women, whose customs were so unfamiliar, with fairness and honesty and they in turn responded with a loyalty that never wavered over the forty-one years he was in office. In one election there were a number of individuals eligible to vote, but who could not read English. Tony, a man of Polish origin, but with enough English to read the ballot, slipped into the polling booth to ensure that those who could not read voted for my father.

Tonight we are having supper with a neighbour, a man whose parents emigrated from Poland. He's Roman Catholic, married to a woman who is English in origin and Anglican. Forty years ago we would have served roast beef, overdone, with mashed potatoes, peas and carrots, that is, if we had eaten together at all. Or if they had even been married to one another. But things have changed.

We are having sausage and cabbage rolls; for five years I have been learning how to make them, asking the babas for their secrets. Annie said to use Chinese cabbage; it's more tender. Alice said use lots of butter. Chop the onions fine. Put in some bacon. Katy said use some dill. I don't use dill but I add a little Chinese fish sauce for flavour with the garlic. My rolls are not well–shaped, not tight little bundles that snuggle together in the pot like the ones Olga makes, but my friend says they taste as good as any cabbage roll he's ever tasted.

# a letter received

Our writing began quite by accident.

Living on a farm fourteen miles from town meant that access to girls was limited. Those that were available were more like sisters, too familiar to be acceptable. Equally difficult was finding some means of obtaining a high school education.

The local country school, a one room affair that had served the community for years, had reached a point where it had neither the resources nor the students to remain viable. The nearest high school lay fourteen miles away, over a road impassable by car for five months of winter. One option was to remain at home and do the work via correspondence. I did most of Grade 9 and 10 in this fashion, completing lessons with my mother's help, and sending the work to a central office for correction and evaluation. The exercise met the requirements of the Department of Education, but allowed for little else, certainly no experiments in a lab or contact with the opposite sex. Only when someone miles away in an office made an error was part of the problem solved.

Work that belonged to another student, a girl my age, was returned to me by mistake. I sent it on to her — Rose was her name — with a note suggesting she might write, which she did. Thus began my first correspondence with a girl. I never met the young woman and our letters ended after a time. I forget what I wrote and remember nothing of what I received in reply, except for one thing: the delightful aroma of her letters, which in her youthful enthusiasm she had doused in perfume. I hope she remembers our writing with the same pleasure I do.

Later at university, though education was now easily accessible and girls even more so, the pleasure of letters did not diminish. Away from home for the first time, while I didn't want to admit it, I was lonely and looked forward to a letter containing a reassuring word from a parent, not to mention cash for the month ahead. Mother wrote the letters. Apart from a brief note on one occasion, I don't remember ever receiving a letter from my father. I heard from him through Mother and in turn, he knew what was happening to me through her. I have never been sure why this was so, but I suspect it was true for many other men as well. Our mothers were placed in the role of messenger. The strange thing about it all was that my father and I understood one another very well, and we developed a close relationship.

I still remember the manner in which letters arrived at university. I lived in a dormitory with eighty other young men. The mailbox consisted of pigeon holes on the wall, arranged in alphabetical order. Each morning at about 10 a.m. the mailman would arrive and leave the mail with the office secretary. She was a good and kind person who, in addition to being the office manager, appeared to have her mind set on finding a husband among the older students. Some of her habits, if not her looks, assured that this was never to happen. Among other things, she had a constipated way of doing things, especially when it came to our mail. She would sort it, then have coffee or type a letter before coming up the stairs to the pigeon holes where, slowly, she would deposit each item in its box. Any effort to hurry her or to take a letter from a box before she was through brought a severe reprimand. At some intuitive level she knew the power she held in her hands and she played it out, one letter at a time. I believe it fortunate she never married.

One of the most memorable letters I received arrived in February, 1965. I recall waiting until just after eleven in the morning when I knew the mail would be sorted before going to the post office. The weather was bitterly cold with a west wind that forced me to walk backwards most of the way, shielding my face in my mitts. For two weeks I had been expecting this letter, but each morning I had been disappointed. On this morning, when I opened the box, it lay there, alone, one legal size envelope postmarked Berkeley. A sticker read Via Air Mail. I took it from the box, hesitated, afraid to open it, fearful of what it might say.

I had come to the town four years previously as the United Church minister. After a year alone, I had married, and Norma and I settled easily into the life of the community. Our son was born there. Having lived in Saskatchewan all my life I knew the country and understood the people. I had been invited to go hunting in the fall and shot my first and last deer there. A local man asked me to curl on his rink in a bonspiel —a sure sign that I had arrived. As far as church life was concerned, we had had our differences and I had made mistakes, but overall it had been a good four years. Yet, for a number of reasons, I knew I could not stay.

Unrest with rural life, the ways of a small town and its church, combined with my own confusion as to who I was and what I wanted, left me dissatisfied. The option of moving to another community and another church, the geographic cure to which clergy become addicted, held no appeal. Instead, I would go back to school, a more satisfying addiction and a far easier reason to give for moving than to say one is bored and confused. After exploring various options, I had placed all my hopes on a year at Berkeley. Letters had been exchanged, a résumé and application submitted. All that remained was a letter of acceptance. Or rejection.

I began to tuck the letter into my parka, then stopped, a voice saying I had best get the bad news over with. Ripping open the letter, I unfolded a single sheet of expensive paper, the kind you can see a watermark in when you hold it up to the light. My eyes raced over the page taking in only the words that mattered: "Have considered ... happy to tell you ... favourable ... " I remember one mistake in the letter, a typo that read "You will begin classes in the fa;;." Mrs. Dye, the typist — and a perfectionist, as I was to later learn — had twice missed being perfect by one key. Even now when I read it, I feel again the pleasure and a deep measure of gratitude for the years which that letter marked an opening.

I wish I had kept more letters, the perfumed pages from the girl I never met, ones my wife wrote to me before we were married, others from my mother. And one from my brother written when I was a long way from home and had failed second year university. Knowing Mother would be devastated, he had written to encourage me, saying it wasn't the end of the world and Mother would get over it.

Lately I have begun keeping letters. Those from my daughter, more cards than letters, are small and delicate. One such creation, a piece of paper, which she made herself, soft blue and pink, carries a hand print-ed quote: "Barlach wrote of God that he conceals himself behind everything and in everything there are narrow cracks through which he ... shines and flashes ... cracks so fine we can never find them again if we only turn our head." On another she drew a small clown-like fig-ure wearing a peculiar hat, an image suggestive of a clown. The note reads: "You realize, of course, that there are not many people who live to be your age ... and still act the way you do." There were times when I know other letters could have been written, but such times have faded like perfume, serving only to make the words of affection all the more memorable.

My son, who has found it difficult to make himself heard in our family, especially with me, discovered that, like myself, he can write what he cannot say. He could have written of the painful times, but rather chose to allude to the struggles and long journey he has been on. Quite apart from me, in ways I could never have imagined, he has been purged of the hurts and disappointments that collected. It is written.

Age has taught me to keep letters, made me realize how important it is to save certain words so I can take them out again, or come upon them by surprise, and let them do their work. Whether it be one waiting in the mail or an old one found at the bottom of a shoe box, even the memory of one, a letter opens the door to my isolation — from the outside.

# August

a holiday
filled with berry picking
unexpected visitors
red wine and conversation
eased the bonds of order
made jesters of us all
we laughed at old stories
told a dozen times before
toasted the bishop and the queen
sure our mothers would not approve

empty glasses, crumpled napkins
two burned out candles keeping watch
a kind of beauty
in the devastation of a finished meal
guests slip away
leaving evening shadows
in the silence of the streets
this day has been tipped on end
poured out
relieved
of all expectations

# coming home

Growing up on a farm, I thought I appreciated the land, that I had a feel for it. "The prairies," like "the coast" or "the mountains," is really shorthand, a code for distance, skylines at sunset, sun and wind, gophers that stand up like sticks in April and assure you winter is over. But there are things you can overlook.

"The land" took on a whole new meaning after a trip to Costa Rica.

If the prairies means space, the ribbon of land that is Costa Rica spells enclosure; walls and canopy made up of every kind of plant and tree, green on green, all squeezed between two oceans. Orchids and hibiscus grow like dandelions. I stood in the midst of hummingbirds, fluorescent greens and blues and shades of red; so many so close, I felt saturated with the little creatures. I managed to spot a Resplendent Quetzel, a parrot-like bird, so named because of his vivid red breast complimented by blue tail feathers, two of them a foot long, falling down like paper streamers. All of this against a backdrop of sound: howler monkeys, strange bird calls, and insect chatter. A *cha cha*. A woman who dresses for Saturday night and dances the tango at mass Sunday morning.

I have travelled a fair bit. There's an excitement in it. The anticipation of something new, unknown. Ordering the tickets. Departure. Incidents unplanned. Like breakfast in Turkey where we had mutton soup — even my wife Norma couldn't eat it. Or the delightful restaurant in Italy where someone gave us a bottle of wine for the balloon sculptures I made. But beyond the adventures, more important even than the clothes and recipes you bring home, certainly more remembered than the pictures you store away in the closet, is the effect on home itself.

For instance, until Costa Rica I never took much interest in birds. I could tell a robin from a crow, and shot sparrows by the dozens. But things have changed. Or maybe it's just that I'm getting older and observing is more my speed. Whatever the case, I see birds now, different birds and differences in birds, details I missed before. I even feed the sparrows now.

We have a Purple Martin colony here, one of the best in the country. As near as I can tell eight pairs nested last summer in our house alone. Three tree swallow families took up residence nearby. Our pride and joy was the pair of flickers that managed to raise two young in the house we built. I made the houses, two of them, and put them up on poplar trees. The flickers inspected them, but didn't build. Then Norma read that if you filled the house with sawdust the flickers would build; the sawdust-filled box resembling an old tree in which they could dig a hole. Sure enough, they took over, pitched sawdust out for a week and settled in, nesting along with the warblers, the robins, and the orioles. Too many sparrows to count. Barn swallows. Bossy little wrens. Kingbirds. Sparrow hawks and starlings reminded us that nature has a way of keeping balance. It occurs to me as I write this that within a radius of a few hundred feet from where I sit there must be at least seventy-five bird families working flat out, making love, building houses, raising kids — all in the space of 12–15 weeks. Orioles are here and gone in less than ten.

But I suppose I have come to most appreciate the winter birds, creatures I never knew existed. Redpolls, there were fourteen of them on a bitter day in January, along with one nuthatch, a few delighted chickadees, one downy woodpecker, the usual crowd of sparrows, and the ever faithful magpie. We have seen junkos and pine grosbeaks. It comes as a bit of a surprise that they all should choose this part of the world. Why wouldn't they — why wouldn't anyone — opt for Costa Rica or California?

There was something else I noticed in Costa Rica. In a bird preserve I saw the most exotic of birds but, in almost every case, there was a message: "These birds are under severe pressure." Or "These birds are endangered." The reasons — deforestation or rich twits buying the birds — illegally — for pets. I knew all this to be true before, but seeing it up close left me with feelings I want to run away from. But it's hard to run.

Someone wrote that the assault on the prairie a hundred years ago was as devastating to this fragile environment as the assault now occurring on the rain forests of South America. Perhaps an overstatement, but certainly not without validity. There's a sadness across the prairie, brought on, it would appear, by low prices and trade wars, economics over which we have little control. But the mood runs deeper, a melancholy that senses something has been lost, a trust broken, that no amount of tinkering will fix, no amount of dollars restore.

Coming home does this to you. It's like hearing strains of music you hadn't listened to before. Seeing a woman in the hall that you hadn't noticed — or maybe she was a bit intimidating, but now you see her sitting against the wall, wearing a purple velvet dress. You ask her for a dance, an old time waltz on a violin, and she accepts. She dances superbly, and you murmur in her ear, "I never knew you."

# Qu'Appelle

An Oblate priest has established a prayer house on the edge of the Qu'Appelle, overlooking Echo Lake, one of five such lakes strung out along the floor of the valley. The Qu'Appelle, "who calls" in French, gains its name from a touching love story involving a young Indian man. Returning home by canoe to meet his loved one, he hears his name being called. Only when he arrives does he learn that the young woman has died the day before; the voice he has heard is hers, calling to him of her death and her love.

It's here that my friend has built a house of prayer. And it was here that Norma and I went to visit one weekend. Nothing special, just a stop to see friends, inspect the prayer house, and enjoy the valley. But for some reason I remember that visit apart from any number of other such trips we have taken. Three events in particular stand out, all occurring within less than twelve hours.

There was nothing elaborate about the rooms — twelve feet square, fifteen at most, one door, a window, white painted walls. But there was something different, different and right. A soft curtain held neatly in a tieback, one chair at a table where you can imagine yourself writing to a friend in the early morning. Or writing your wife to say the marriage is over. Bedspreads, folds of blue, mauve, and pink, invite you to bury yourself and fade into dreaming. A Celtic cross, perhaps a gift from some

Druid priest, hangs in the stairwell. The place feels more like an English B & B at the edge of a village than a small-town hotel. Or maybe a retreat house where a monk will ring the bell for prayers at seven and set break-fast out at eight. You can pray if you want and eat when it pleases you. Or sleep. And be all alone.

Down below, at first glance, the place looks like a small town bar. Several people sit drinking and laughing. Three old timers, the "regulars" with two day whiskers and a cigarette, sip their beer. Two women in shorts perch on the railing, entertaining a young man who seems well on his way to be being drunk. Yet, even here, there is evidence that the same hand, whose presence has touched the upstairs, has been at work. The "regulars" nod a greeting and look almost clean. You can breathe the air and risk sitting down at a table without sticking to it. A newly painted sign above the door has a ring of poetry to it: "The Calling Lakes Hotel." We find chairs and order a pitcher of beer. I had not seen the place before Kathy took over, but I knew what it had been like.

Small town prairie hotels were all the same: two-story, wood frame boxes painted white or drab yellow, like a stained tooth in an ugly mouth. Out front the sign read "Hotel." There were rooms upstairs, but I don't remember much about them, just the beer parlour downstairs, or "Licensed Premises" as the words said on the frosted window. I do remember the dirty white door, the paint worn off around the door knob, boot marks kicked into the bottom. In summer, the tear in the screen door let the cat out and the flies in. On occasion you could stand at the door and look in, even sneak all the way in, until spotted and chased out. The room varied only slightly from one establishment to the next. Usually there were plywood stacking chairs and arborite topped tables, scarred brown at the edges from cigarettes left burning by someone too drunk to notice. Foot-square, beige tile covered the floor, the pattern worn off in front of the bar and the bathroom door.

Two things in particular about beer parlours never changed: the customers and the smell. An unmistakable stench of mingled sweat, spilled beer, smoke, and urine from the toilets seeped into carpets, wall paper, furniture, and clothes. The clientele, entirely men up until the early 1960s, had as their primary goal to get drunk and then, by the end

The Kenaston Hotel looks little different now than it did 60 years ago.
Every town had one. Their main function was to provide a "licensed
premises", better known as the beer parlour.

of the day, wander home in a stupor, smelling much like the beer parlour they left behind.

Parlour, premises — I am struck now by the elegance of these
terms, so very English and proper in tone. In fact, the term *beer parlour*
became a kind of profanity for most wives, words spit rather than spoken. It was the centre of activity for the hotel, indeed for the whole village where men of the community settled down for an afternoon or
evening of drinking, while their families waited outside in the car.

I remembered all this and wondered what would possess a thirty-five
year old single woman to leave behind a teaching position, eleven
years of experience, and a comfortable house to buy such a place.

"You have courage," my friend commented.

"No, I don't think so," Kathy laughed, a look of surprise and
delight on her face. "It's what I've always wanted to do."

Its peaked grey roof stands at least thirty feet in the air. An immense steeple rises above it, topped with a cross. Old trees, several feet in circumference, taller than anything I have seen on the prairies before, keep watch above the grounds and cemetery. Headstones, the majority of them bearing French names, mark deaths as far back as 1880. Many of the stones are spotted with moss; a few, as if tired, tilt at precarious angles. On one appears the names of four children, all from one family, the oldest nineteen and the youngest eight months.

For a moment, in the midst of the gravestones, shaded from the sun by the church, I imagine a little piece of France has been carried across the sea and settled here, a bit of Europe carved out of an Indian reserve, hanging onto existence in a prairie town of pickup trucks, old brick houses, and one rundown store.

Up the street a block are some of the last remaining figures who made it all possible; three elderly nuns living in a house that once housed a dozen active sisters. Just the day before, a fourth sister, over ninety years of age, had awakened in the morning and told the cook that she was going to die. The cook, a younger woman, had the good sense not to call a doctor or ambulance, but suggested to the old sister she should get into her pyjamas and lie down; pyjamas and bed were better for dying. Later, the other sisters and the cook gathered around her bed. One of them anointed the old woman with oil. When they checked her in the evening she was dead.

We were sitting in the Shell station café waiting for our Sunday breakfast, watching the locals, when Robert came in. He was a good-looking man, six-feet tall, neat in his dark suit and tie. He had the kind of bearing that, from the moment he entered the room, he owned the place. The lines on his face suggested that somewhere along the way there must have been a fair bit of pain. But today there is laughter on his face, a kind of give-her-hell look, and a glint in his eye.

He recognized my friend, the priest, and stopped to talk. Robert and his wife had just come from church. The mass, Robert tells us, was good and the preacher gave them a fine homily. Best homily he has heard in a long time. What about? Robert couldn't remember. We all laughed. But it was a very good homily.

"What is it you do here, Robert?"

"Put up farm buildings all over Saskatchewan. We put 'em up from one end to the other. I work with my three sons. Figure out how to manage that, you tell me!"

"How did you get such a business?"

"Long story. I ran a hotel at the Peace Gardens, you know where that is at Boissevain? Well, I did that for ten years, started it more on a dare. Made a success of it. I knew the industry. But after ten years it nearly destroyed me. So I sold it. I haven't had a drink in twenty-two years. I had three sons and they wanted to go into this business. We looked around and I was headed for Camrose, Alberta where we were going to start up. Stopped here for gas. We were out on the road again and that car just turned around and came back. And we've been here ever since, putting up farm buildings all over Saskatchewan.

"I don't exaggerate my stories. Just ask my wife. This is the truth. We left here for Alberta and somehow that car just turned around. It was like a voice said I was meant to be here."

Historians have cast doubt on the story of how the Qu'Appelle received its name. No one really knows how the story began. Early records make no mention of the young man hearing his lover call him. It's simply a tale someone started, which grew into legend, assisted in no small way by the native poet Pauline Johnson who told the story in a poem, "The Legend of the Qu'Appelle Valley." Like every good story, this one has gained a little in the telling.

And yet ...

There's a part of me that resists dismissing the story. In a day when every hero must be brought low, every mystery explained, when everything lies scattered and the soul has trouble putting its pieces together, I need stories like this one of how love and love denied gave a valley its name. To this day young women dream and old women are visited by premonitions. Priests build prayer houses and men hear voices telling them this is home.

# dirt

The spring had been dry and the winds severe. The topsoil was beginning to drift in the fields. A film of dust settled in the milk pitcher left open on the table, on clean clothes on the line, and ground on the kitchen floor beneath your shoe. In mid-afternoon a great, dark cloud formed in the west, not a thunderhead, but a wall of black that extended high in the air and hung there, then crept slowly across the fields. I can still see the dread in my father's eyes. "I've seen those bastards before," was all he said.

The "bastards" to which he referred were the dust storms of the Great Depression, a period of time that extended for roughly ten years between 1929 and 1939. In Saskatchewan we called it "the Dirty Thirties," an event that doesn't rate in magnitude with the tragedy of WW I or the horror of the Irish famine. Yet, for my parents and their generation, having known good times only to see everything blow away, the Dirty Thirties were a devastation like none other. I didn't witness these events first hand, but the signs were still there in my day. In the rough, rolling land where we lived, the tops of the hills remain to this day whitish-grey, like old men gone bald, the result of years of erosion from water but especially the bastards, the winds that never stop.

The Dirty Thirties, however, as damaging as they were to the land, were about more than just the good black earth that filled the ditches or sifted through the windows. The wind and heat left other wounds, which in time healed, but the scars remained.

"Be careful, you never know…" she would say, and the words would trail off. To her dying day my mother, though she had quite enough to live on, feared poverty. Of course, she had every reason to. Too many crops had failed, too many dreams had faded. To be cautious, to not enjoy oneself too much, was a protection against getting your hopes up and having them dashed. Patrick Kavanaugh, the Irish poet who was raised in the poverty of rural Ireland, said that it was not the lack of life's necessities that made poverty so difficult, it was what happened at the deeper level of the spirit. My mother's spirit didn't die in the Dirty Thirties, but it was a damn close.

"Get the team and Bennett Buggy," Father would say. On other occasions, it would be, "Get the team and democrat." At the time, I understood that I was to hitch the horses to a light wagon with four wheels and a seat at the front for two. Later I came to appreciate the origin of the names and the kind of gallows humour attached to both titles.

The prime minister of Canada in the early 1930s was one R.B. Bennett, a man more unlucky than inept. While he accomplished some good things, the Depression overtook him to the point that he became the focal point of the country's anger. He was to leave behind at least one enduring symbol. As hard times continued, farmers without money to pay for gas removed the motors from their cars, cut the chassis down, and hitched horses to the front creating a dependable even if less dignified, means of travel — the "Bennett Buggy." Democrat had a somewhat different origin.

In the U.S., in the days before automobiles, the carriage could be a quite elegant affair and as such was identified with people of status and wealth. The common citizen required something less expensive. And so was born "the democrat": a light weight wagon, the Volkswagen of its day, a vehicle with no frills pulled by two horses. Or in Saskatchewan in the 1930s, where the political climate was somewhat different, it could be a Bennett Buggy, depending on my father's preference.

The son of a neighbouring family fell ill and was placed in hospital, twenty miles away. The child's mother and my mother took our '28 Chevy, with just enough gas for the trip to visit the boy. After seeing the child, they decided they should stop at the Owl café, a Chinese establishment, and "splurge" just a little. Between them they had ten cents to buy two ice cream cones.

The Irish poet Brendan Behan said, "During the depression drunkenness was not a social disgrace ... to get enough to eat was an achievement. To get drunk was a victory." My father, and many men like him, required an ever increasing number of victories to keep going.

1937. The municipal office, the centre of local government. Present is a municipal counsellor, one Glen Nichols, my father who is reeve of the municipality, and a third man, a constituent of Glen Nichols. The man has requested thirty bushels of oats, which he claims he needs for seed. Glen doubts the man's honesty, believing that he will use the oats to feed his horses, but, cagey fellow that he is and ever the politician, he decides to be on the safe side and offers the man fifteen bushels instead. The man, knowing his honesty is being questioned, begins to curse, calling Glen every name in the book. As a final shot he shouts, "You can take your fifteen bushels of oats and shove them up your arse!" then storms out, slamming the door behind him. There is a brief silence, Glen turns to my father and says, "God, Alex, I'm glad I didn't give him thirty."

I think she was only five years old. Her family lived on a farm a few miles away. Her parents were immigrants from eastern Europe. I never saw the child, but heard my mother and father speak of her. Word came that she had died, and my parents went to the home to sit with the family. When they returned, I remember them saying that the child had had rickets. They went to the funeral, but were late by five minutes and missed the

An authentic "Bennett Buggy," a car with the motor removed and replaced by old-fashioned horsepower. It was a distant relative of "the Democrat".

service. The priest, because the family were poor and marginal in their support of the Roman Catholic Church had cut the proceedings short. Years later, I looked up rickets. It is a disease brought on by lack of Vitamin D and general malnutrition. Only then did it occur on me that this child's death was due to a slow and continuous state of starvation.

I don't know why she married him, probably to escape something that seemed worse. He was a dark, greasy-looking character. Maybe he was a fine man, but things looked suspicious. They lived in a two-room shack at the far end of nowhere. If she got to town three times a year, she was lucky. They had two children, frightened-looking waifs, like two deer flushed from cover. I remember Father coming home, saying the mother had committed suicide; she had drunk rat poison.

"Alex ... you help me. My wife she dead. Got no money to bury her ... you help me." The man pleads his case, tears welling up in his eyes. The scene has become all too common: a destitute farmer wanting approval for some form of "relief" and my father, reeve of the munici-pality, is the key to it.

"We'll see what we can do." Father pours the man another cup of tea and heads for the phone on the wall, cranks once, and waits. "Give me the municipal office," he barks into the phone, a habit which, like many of his others, Mother has tried to curb, but with little effect.

"Jim, there's a man here needs a few bucks for a funeral. See that he gets it when he comes in." The man leaves, grateful for the help. Such is this man's gratitude and unswerving loyalty, and many others like him, that in the forty-one consecutive years my father is reeve of the municipality, he is elected by acclamation in every election with the exception of five.

Two days later, early in the morning, a fourteen-year-old boy appears at the door. It is the man's son; he has driven the ten miles from his home in an open sleigh. The temperature has dropped to fifteen below and the boy is cold.

"Where are you going?" Mother asks. "To get my mother," he answers. He is heading for town and the railway station, fourteen miles further west. The train will bring the body in a rough box from the city, delivering it to the station where the boy will pick it up. A local furniture maker has constructed a coffin.

Mother prepares the boy a lunch while he warms himself. He will make it to town by noon, rest until the train arrives at two, then turn and head back across the frozen prairie with his mother's body in the back of the sleigh.


1997. We built a new house out of the city where we had a little more space but the soil was poor. I called up a landscaper. Yes, he could supply topsoil — garden mix, regular — whatever I needed and as much as I wanted. In the end, he made three trips with a semi-trailer, delivering thirty yards of rich, black soil.

"The owner bought a half-section north of the city," the driver said. "There used to be a ravine running through it years ago, but in the thirties it filled to a depth of four or five feet with topsoil. All we have to do is dig it out, screen it, and add manure."

If you can believe it, we grew a castor bean seven feet high in that soil, so big I could stand in the shade under it. My wife harvested enough tomatoes to make a years supply of salsa and pizza sauce. No end of peas and corn. Down the slope at the back of the yard, flowers bloomed all summer. There was nothing more satisfying than digging a hole for a tree, or hauling wheelbarrows of earth to build a berm, and ending up with dirt in your clogs, ground into your feet so that it took a week of scrubbing to finally wash away.

I can't help remembering where that dirt came from. Good, black dirt, the same dirt, over which my mother wept and my father cursed.

# a sewer went out to sow

A quilt block in Saskatchewan: there should be nothing surprising about this. Making quilts is as much a part of this country as dust storms and long underwear. But this block was different: a piece of ground, one hundred and forty-one feet square, in the middle of a farmer's field, lying open to the mercy of sun and wind, hoping for rain.

Like all quilt blocks, this one had a pattern: a ten-foot width of flax as a border, triangular sections at the corners growing calendula and borage, sunflowers forming a labyrinth in the middle, and at the very centre a diamond of nasturtiums. I know; I helped measure it out, mark it with stakes and string, and later was one of the foot soldiers fighting a losing battle with the volunteer barley that sprang up, threatening to overwhelm the entire project.

"The quilt," as it came to be known during the course of the summer, was my daughter Suzanne's creation. Inspiration arose, in part, out of her relationship with her grandmother, a pioneer woman who farmed, raised a family, and in her spare time made quilts. Beneath the surface there were other issues — plants and earth, the honouring of women, a deepening appreciation for the land — all woven together in the dreams of an artist.

I have to admit that as the summer progressed I had my doubts as to the success of the quilt, a not surprising development, given the fact that most artistic endeavours in my education occupied a place just above begging. Would music or painting put bread on the table? Actors never amounted to anything. Writing, poetry, even working for a newspaper was no way to live.

They say it's the land and the weather that dried our spirits and left dust in our souls. Partly true. After picking stones and breaking sod, who had energy left for a poem? Or time for those who did? And when you had waited for a crop to grow and the rains didn't come, or hail wiped out whatever did grow, survival took precedence, not a painting or a play. But, as I was to learn, this quilt had a life of its own and an effect on our lives I had not anticipated.

I remember quilts being made in our living room. Father would put the quilting frame together, a rectangle made of four strips of wood the size of a quilt, held together by clamps at each corner. The contraption then rested on four chairs just the right height for six or eight women to sit around while they stitched the previously created quilt blocks to the backing. I would crawl under the frame to play, a safe and hidden place, guarded by a fence of legs and shoes around the perimeter. I remember sitting there trying to determine which voice belonged to which pair of shoes.

Among the quilters there were women noted for their fine, even stitching, a skill much admired by everyone. Modesty forbade the individual to ever take credit for such ability, saying instead that others did just as well or that they would never be as good as their mothers. There were also quilters of lesser ability. One woman created large, uneven stitches that resembled the efforts of a child at play or a husband repairing his shirt. In the interest of community relations, no one said anything, at least not in the woman's presence.

When completed, the quilt was raffled off, usually at a country dance, ten cents a ticket or three for a quarter, all of the proceeds going to the Red Cross in aid of Canada's war effort. One year, an old bachelor won the quilt and the women were disappointed that their hard work would not receive the kind of appreciation it deserved in a bachelor's shack. Beyond the patriotic and the practical, however, there were other motives for quilting.

It's hard to imagine now but from the time the land was settled in the early 1900s until well into the '50s the great majority of farm women spent most of their life within a small circle that extended no further than the local school and the homes of a few neighbours. A trip to town on Saturday provided a change, but when winter came and the roads drifted in, even this outing was denied. Each year Mother ventured to town in mid-December, and then fifty miles by train to the city to do the Christmas shopping. One winter she did not leave the farm again until mid-April when the roads finally opened. Gathering to quilt in someone's home, coupled with monthly Red Cross meetings, was a time out, a place where women created a space for themselves, away from house, children, and husbands — Zorba's equivalent of the full catastrophe. Quilting was a legitimate reason to be on your own and break the isolation.

When my mother was well into her seventies she designed and made a quilt commemorating the province's seventy-fifth anniversary, one of dozens of similar quilts created across the province by individuals and groups. My mother's quilt reflected the manner in which the land had been surveyed. Thirty-six blocks represented the thirty-six sections in a township, each block depicting a particular event or era in the province's history: an Indian tepee, a Mountie, a railroad, an elevator. Other blocks depicted more recent events such as the mining of potash. There were particular blocks representing land set aside for the school and the Hudson's Bay. Quilting, begun for reasons of survival, became for my mother a means by which she claimed her role as an artist, and for the quilt the status of an art form.

It was all of this history, coupled with her own development as an artist, that gave rise to my daughter's quilt.


With the measuring and staking complete, I wondered why we weren't seeding the plot sooner; it was past the first of June and, as every farmer knows, crops must be seeded in May or they will freeze before September. Using a little Roundup beforehand to settle the score with the barley would help. More importantly, if it didn't rain inside of ten days we would have to rig some kind of water system or everything would burn up. But these issues were clearly more of a concern to me than to the artist.

In mid-June, with the seed finally in the ground, my wife and I paid a visit to the block with the intention of doing a bit of weeding. One look at the field and I wanted to turn for home. Volunteer barley, lush and green, some of it a foot high, covered the low spots, obliterating any sign of borage and nasturtiums. The previous year the land had been seeded with barley, a large amount of which had never been harvested and remained in the soil. It was this seed that had now sprouted and created what a friend later suggested might be called a shag carpet rather than a quilt.

We set about attacking the worst of the barley, but soon gave up, estimating that at the rate we were going it would take two weeks to do half the plot; by then a fresh crop would have sprung up behind us. My wife continued weeding, and I settled for hoeing sunflowers, where the barley was not so thick. Suzanne would have to decide what to do with the barley. At this point I was certain the quilt didn't stand a snowball's chance. But a voice reminded me: "This is not your project."

As the weeks passed the flax and calendula struggled. I had no idea what borage looked like. The sunflowers held their own. Rain was limited, but at crucial moments enough fell to keep the plants, and my faint hopes, alive. But what was to be done with the barley? In the best tradition of turning adversity to advantage, Suzanne decided that rather than fight it, a battle we were sure to lose, she would welcome the barley. Weeding it from sections where it was thinner and leaving the heavier of it to grow, she created a wide band of green, which by late summer would turn yellow, a "river of barley" weaving through the block.

A second development proved equally beneficial both in the struggle with the barley and my outlook toward the project.

There began to appear a steady trek of young men and women all intent on weeding and hoeing. One afternoon I arrived to find three women in sunhats, down on their hands and knees, weeding the flax and chatting about the things young women chat about. Tom Sawyer could not have done better. An old grey dog had strayed in and lay on his back cooling himself in the barley. A square of earth with its struggling plants and river of barley had become, like a quilting frame in my mother's living room, the occasion of a communal event.

As the summer progressed, friends would ask, "What's Suzanne doing?" Parents of my generation often mumble when asked such questions, wanting to say their child has been accepted into medicine or law, or is working for an oil company in Calgary. It's the kind of story that was popular when I was setting out, when "getting ahead" was everything, when progress was taken for granted and success the only acceptable result. But that was forty years ago. What do you say now? What do you say when all these easy assumptions are in question? What do you say when your child is an artist and you are pleased she has designed a quilt block overgrown with barley?

"Well, she's working on an art project, a quilt block she designed on a piece of ground sixty miles west of the city. Different plants — flax, sunflowers, borage — will make the pattern and ... " On and on I would go until I learned to stop and listen.

One woman who had seen the block talked with enthusiasm about the plants and how the different textures of each would resemble a quilt. Another had no difficulty associating quilt blocks with plants, the land, and art. One man responded as I had, concerned the plants

An aerial view of the quilt block created by my daughter
in a Saskatchewan field.

would never mature and Roundup would have helped. But in time his outlook began to change as he saw that there was more to the venture than bushels to the acre.

As the fall progressed, the surprises continued. Two reporters travelled from the city to take pictures and write articles that appeared in the local papers. We received phone calls about the project, and a card from a friend saying how much she appreciated the work.

Everything grew and bloomed, but at different times. The barley? A curse, to be sure, but in the end, it looked as if it belonged, turning yellow and forming a distinctive band through the block. Like the stitching of some of the quilters in years past, it was there, part of the picture and, while we would have liked to rid ourselves of it, we could not. In fact, the barley contributed more to our conversation than did the flax or borage. The sunflowers did very well, so well that Suzanne picked over five hundred of them and sold them at a street fair. I couldn't see why anyone would buy sunflowers and certainly not at the price she was asking. In the end she sold $300 worth. Not only that, she was offered a contract to design and create something similar for a town in the south of the province as part of their arts centre.

A quilt created by my mother depicting the history of Saskatchewn, beginning in the lower right and progressing to the upper left.

The quilt did not materialize last summer as planned; the weather and the barley saw to that. Certainly, it was not what I had in mind. Yet, it succeeded with the kind of success only the artist can be fool enough to wait on.

The project gathered us: a little army of weeders, an old dog, my wife and I, two reporters, numerous friends with whom we talked, the readers in the newspapers. It is as if we had been waiting, tired of the long winter, tired of the same faces, tired of being closed in, needing to get out, wanting to talk to someone different, do something foolish for a day, and when asked what we had done say, "We made a quilt in the middle of a farmer's field with flax, borage, a labyrinth of sunflowers, some nasturtiums at the centre, with a river of barley running through the middle."

# glory, glory how peculiar

I first met Terry when we were students studying theology in preparation for ordination. Everything about him, from the quick movements
of his body to his pencil thin moustache, was neat, tidy, and carried an
air of authority. He had been a boxing champion in the navy and
rumour had it that few opponents had ever beaten him. I knew from
the beginning that he was in charge. At cribbage he always found a way
to win. In an argument, if he were losing, he could raise some issue
quite unrelated to the subject then slip away untouched. But for all this
we were friends.

He was older, had ridden the rails in the 30s, survived six years of
war as a sailor, worked eight years as a fireman, a man searching for
what had been lost while I was a youth of twenty, confused, trying to
grow up, searching for what was yet to come. In retrospect I am sure I
found in him much of what I admired and relied on in my father.

As for theology the two of us were unlikely prospects.

"Evans," he would say, "see that woman over there with the broad
hips? They get like that from bearing children and other things. You
never thought of that, did you?"

"No, can't say as I have."

"You need to know these things. Work it into your next essay on
Jesus and the Kingdom of God."

In 1961, we were ordained together. In the next thirty years we did
not write and saw one another only twice. He went to Newfoundland,

then to Ontario, and finally retired in Nova Scotia. I stayed in Saskatchewan, moved to California, then moved back to Saskatchewan. Three years ago, he came west for a visit. We met over lunch, and for two hours it was as if we had been apart no more than a week. History was brought up-to-date. We told our stories, bragged a little, reviewed all the scandals among old friends.

Four months ago he came west again. Over coffee he told me he was ill and if nature or an experimental medication did not stop the disease, he had two years, at most, to live. I told him about my prostate biopsy.

"It's like having a staple gun go off, firing needles, only this time it's up your backside along with half the other equipment in the doctor's office." There was a little bravado in our stories, the kind of thing you do to keep your thoughts in check.

As the afternoon ended, I said I wanted to buy his lunch. "Okay, good", he said. "If I am alive in two years we can meet and I'll pay. And if I'm not, then you can say one of the last things you did for this old bugger was buy him lunch." We laughed and did not notice that we were twenty years apart in age.

Four weeks later Terry's brother called. I knew what it was about before he told me. Medication had destroyed Terry's immune system. There was some suggestion that a doctor had missed a diagnosis. Whatever the case, Terry came down with a cold, then pneumonia, and died within six days. He had planned his funeral with military precision. He had told his wife that he was to be cremated and his ashes sent back to Saskatchewan. There was to be a memorial service at which another friend and I would lead the service. Tears came to my eyes; a rare gift had been given, and I was pleased to receive it.

The memorial proceeded as these events usually do. Terry had requested "The Battle Hymn of The Republic" as one of the hymns, a fine piece of music, but one which suits a parade or a revolt better than a funeral. I was prepared to live with it until Terry's brother stated he didn't like the hymn either.

"But Terry requested it," countered a sister, an argument that usually silences everyone when funerals are being planned, no matter how awful the request may be.

"Yes, but he won't be here," the brother shot back.

Inwardly I gave a small cheer, and suggested we choose another hymn. I must admit I took some slight satisfaction in doing something other than Terry requested. They selected "Blest Be the Tie That Binds," whereupon I began to wish we had stayed with the original request.

Later that week, family and friends gathered at the church. The soloist sang "Amazing Grace." A eulogy dragged on twice as long as it needed to. We lit a candle. The other preacher and I said all the necessary things, and people wept and laughed. We had lunch in the basement: crackers and cheese, and sticky squares that several people said were the best they'd ever tasted. After lunch we drove fifteen miles into the countryside to a cemetery where we put the urn into a foot square hole in the ground. The site was less than a mile from where Terry grew up.

Later, in twos and threes, we walked, reading the names on the tombstones, and recalling stories about some of the people. Someone noticed that the same family name appeared at different places throughout the graveyard. "Yeah, well, any closer than that and they couldn't stand one another," one of the old men remarked.

As I drove away, I looked back. A cluster of roses stood out, deep red against the earth and withered grass. Stubble and summer fallow fields rolled away to the skyline, a patchwork carpet in faded shades of brown and yellow.

# in the space between

Along with the onions and the corn, the carrot tops have faded, grown tired you might say. Gone is the lush growth of May and June when beginning was everything , each new shoot a sign of progress. Bumping about from flower to flower, the bumblebee seems slower than a month ago. It happens every year in late August; a stillness descends, like that of a cemetery where gravestones, dates, and verses forgotten in the moss, seem possessed of a peculiar speech. A presence more than substance, a memory carried in sound, smell, and shadow. Such a quiet arrived in the garden today. It was as if some internal clock, unnoticed in the rush of summer, had once more made its movement felt; a sixth sense at work.

Here on the prairie, seasons change in a day and, like a kiss of friendship from a Russian or a bow of greeting from a Japanese, every conversation must begin with the weather. But this time, this unannounced arrival in my garden, is different yet again from fall or summer. It has none of winter's edge or spring's abandon; it is time between, a space that sets memory in motion.


Fall. Harvest has begun. Because the day has been hot and dry we will work late into the night. Darkness as black as the Earl of Hell's riding boot, in the words of an old Irish neighbour, covers the farm, the hills, and fields. Against the faint light of a million stars stand the silhouettes of the house and barn. A square of light thrown from the kitchen window hangs, suspended, brave and insignificant against the night that surrounds it. Far to the south, across the stubble field, appears a spot of yellow, visible for a time, then gone, only to reappear in a moment. It is as if a space ship has lost its way in the middle of our field. But this is no alien; it is Father on the combine. In minutes he will be stopped, impatient, waiting on the truck to unload the grain.

There were some thankless tasks on a farm: cleaning pig pens and picking stone are two that come to mind. But there were other jobs that made it all worthwhile: cutting hay with a good mower and a sharp knife, watching a three foot stand of slough grass falling soft and even like pages in a book. But the best job of all was hauling grain, chasing down a combine in a half-ton truck across stubble fields in the dead of night. Pull in close and stop. Shout a few words above the motor and the rattle of the auger. Wait for the box to fill, then turn for the granary. Something solid and good about ninety bushels of wheat and an old truck growling along in bull low. Clean work. Satisfying. A strange exhilaration, all alone in the night.

For some reason fall is filled with memories like this. Maybe it's the colours. Or the food that fall brought forth. The best meal going was fresh corn on the cob and "spring chicken," young birds hatched in April and raised like pets by my mother. She would fatten a half dozen of them and on a Saturday afternoon have Father "stick" them , a messy business of blood and feathers one sought to avoid. On Sunday afternoon she dipped the cut pieces in egg and bread crumbs, then fried them in butter. Friends and relatives would arrive, Herb Edwards with a bottle of whisky along with Carl Weckerling, a bachelor who craved good pie and ice cream. My aunt came from the city and brought cake. A great feast it was. A celebration.

But fall has not yet come. It will be here tomorrow or in a week, after the first frost when the leaves begin to drop. But not yet. I am reminded again of how easy it is to rush on, of how difficult it is to remain "in between." I am uncomfortable; no, more than that. To try and stay within this little space of time brings with it a fine edged fear. There is something here I cannot control, cannot name. How anxious I am to fill the void, to close what lies open.

Premature. The sex manuals, in the days when I had cause to read them, diagnosed the problem of being premature. Stress. Anxiety. Fear. All the issues therapists find easy to talk about and prescribe. But how do you diagnose and prescribe that which has no name? A premonition. And a premonition is different than being premature.

But frightened of what? The fury of a summer storm brings with it a particular fear as does a visit to the doctor. But this fear is different. It can shiver your belly on a hot day. It lies just beyond awe and wonder, a moment when one is both terrified and fascinated, left groping for speech and knowing none will be sufficient. Such a confusion of feeling can erupt at any time. At a funeral or a wedding. In a garden at the end of summer.

Some years ago we visited Vimy Memorial, the monument erected at Vimy, France, to honour Canadian soldiers who died in WW I and especially at the Vimy battle itself. I cannot imagine how terrible that war must have been. Any war. But WW I seems particularly savage. After over three years of fighting, the armies of the English and the French, our colonial mothers, had been near bled to death. Someone said Vimy Ridge was important and had to be taken. The English had failed. So let the Canadians try, the colonials, the same ones who, at the beginning of the war, the English government had thought should be commanded by English officers. The colonials succeeded brilliantly, driving the enemy from the ridge and holding the ground. The overall offensive, from a military stand point, achieved little.

Years after, a Canadian architect and artist named Walter Allward was commissioned to design and build the monument. The effort was to take over ten years and would result in a work of rare beauty. Twin pillars soar 226 feet into the sky above the French countryside. Some twenty figures, carved into white marble, are marked by simple dignity and grace. On the walls appear "the missing": 11,285 names in all, chiselled in the stone with meticulous care. These are the men blown to pieces and never found. Not far away are trenches and tunnels and countless scraps of battle preserved as a faint reminder of the mud and din of war. They say it was at Vimy Ridge that Canada became a nation. Out of a dreadful battle we came to know our identity. A different time.

I learned a word for all this a few years back in a course that was really quite boring and from which I cannot remember another solitary thing. But I remember one word: *liminal*. A good word I thought. It rolls off your tongue with a bit of a rumble, like it is going somewhere. Liminal has to do with *limen*, a word which originally referred to the cross piece or the threshold of a doorway. Hence *liminality* has come to mean in between, part way, a time of transition. In psychology and medicine, liminality refers to the threshold of consciousness, the point below which a stimulus is not perceived. One is affected, the senses disturbed, but at a level which the mind does not register. Sub-liminal messages. In advertising such methods are banned, but nature persists.

In liminal time we find ourselves caught, in between, a foot in two camps. Affected by many forces we could go either way. Most disturbing of all, we are largely unaware of these forces and their effect. It follows, therefore, that in liminal time we are not in control. Confirmation of this comes from those who have passed through a crisis such as divorce or illness: control lies elsewhere. Such time, therefore, is fraught with danger and burdened with promise. In some small way, even in my garden watching the bee and the corn, it is so. What am I to do? Hang onto summer or embrace the fall? Every parent who has lost a child, or spouse whose mate has died, will tell you of a terrible struggle: to go on when every bone and nerve says turn back. Family, church, and work, even my own mind, say I must go on. But the heart says stay, leave the room as it was, the memories intact, unexamined. Turn back to a world that was. Such is liminal time when we are bombarded with memories and feelings of which our mind knows little.

How shall we live between the times? The liminal state for an individual, for a church, or a country is like a great plateau, a sweep of prairie stretching into sky without familiar landmarks. I do not know how to read the new markers. A demanding time like no other. The assumption in this culture is that one must act. Like that peculiar little mouse that keeps jumping in all directions as a means of survival, one is expected to keep moving, mere activity mistaken for a valid response.

There exists a third option, to neither turn back nor leap forward, but rather to remain. In liminal space, we are asked to wait; stay here awhile to see and hear. To not jump one way or the other, however, is difficult.

Just this morning there was news that a small delegation from Canada had gone to Texas in an effort to have the governor commute the death sentence of a Canadian scheduled to die in four days. There is clear evidence he did not receive a fair trial, not to mention the fact that Texas, having executed dozens of people in the past ten years, continues to have a high murder rate. To raise such issues in such a bold fashion accomplishes two things. It places the individuals who have raised their voices in dissent in a vulnerable position; they must stand alone, identified in a less than friendly environment. Beyond this, however, their actions raise troubling questions. Is it right to kill another person who may be innocent of the crime he is accused? More difficult still: is it right to kill another person even if guilty?

It is no simple matter to enter liminal space, and having done so, bear the cost. Not many votes to be had "in between." Or as my friend Raymond says, you don't get invited to many parties. But liminal time is not nothing. Above all it is not bad, wrong, sinful, insignificant. Only different. Nelson Mandela could wait twenty-seven years. David Milgaard, convicted of rape and murder, spent twenty-three years in the no man's land of prison, and would surely have died if we had had the death penalty. His mother entered that same space, and fought until her son was found innocent and released.

So ... we continue earning a living, and paying the bills. Tending to the garden provides a kind of stability. It is time to be diligent in listening and also in speaking. I find it essential to write. A friend commented in a letter awhile ago, "It is important when we see something, feel something about ourselves ... that we do whatever it is (like writing to someone) that keeps it from disappearing, just becoming a faint memory of something that passed through our life." One's musings, half-formed thoughts, must find some place of expression. It is the way creation continues, the way we continue, in this time between.

Through it all I endeavour to remember that there remains moments for celebration. Just now a friend in Kamloops phoned to talk. He said the rates were cheaper before eight. We both knew it was a way of tending the garden we began over twenty years ago. Next week I must get up early and go to breakfast with friends, an outing that resumes with the arrival of September. The same waitress, the same special. Harold will have his eggs over easy with hash browns. I may splurge and have a tea cake with my muffin. And what of the garden?

Tomorrow the bumblebee will have gone and the air will be such that there will be no doubt fall has come.

# what name shall we give this child

One Eyed Bill. Windy Martin. Harrow Pin Joe. No mother would ever give her child such a name; they must be acquired through a process of naming, a kind of secular christening that picks up on a personal trait or an event in an individual's life. After all, a name bestows an identity for life.

Albert lived in our community when I was a child and was known by all as a great talker. One day Bill met Albert on the street and, without thinking, greeted him with, "Hello Windy, how are ya?" A fist fight broke out as Albert sought to defend his honour but to no avail; he was Windy from that day on. Joe was a farmer my father spoke of who put harrow pins into the rear end of dressed turkeys to increase their weight and was ever after known as Harrow Pin Joe. One Eyed Bill runs a garage in town. He came by the name the day a piece of steel flew from a chisel and took out his right eye.

I have become interested in this naming process after discovering I may have acquired a title myself. Here at the lake I suspect I am known as "the preacher" and my house is "the preacher's house." I know my neighbour, retired from university, is known as "the professor" and his house is "the professor's house." There is another fellow who has various adjectives applied to him: "the jerk," "crazy old George" or, if not a particular title then a shake of the head, sometimes accompanied by a profanity, precedes the utterance of his name. I have been wondering how he feels having gone through life being looked upon in such derogatory terms. Of course, he probably doesn't realize this is happening. Or possibly he does, but has become accustomed to it, accepting what seems to be ridicule as a kind of affection. Which gives me pause for thought.

What if I'm in the same boat as George the Jerk, in possession of a title far more derogatory than preacher, but no one dares speak of it to my face? I can't possibly think of what it could be. Of course, this is not surprising; such names arise out of some aspect of our being which we prefer to remain unaware of, but others see and apply a name. In my younger years the idea that I could be so unaware, or that anyone thought poorly of me, would have been devastating, but now it is not quite as troubling. I once had a student from Tanzania who, when a discussion of homosexuality arose, shook his head in apparent confusion. "In my country we have no word for such a thing," he said.

No name; no existence.

My father's name was John Alexander Evans, Alex for short. He was a big man, six feet, over two hundred pounds, with huge hands. The ring he wore was so large someone said that it looked like a horse collar. And he had a personality to match. Such was his nature that he was at his best in the midst of crisis, preferably someone else's; his own he didn't handle as well. Only in later years did I appreciate that wherever I went as a child my father had broken trail ahead of me. Even if the old men and women didn't know my name, they always knew I was "Alex's son." But sooner or later you have to earn a name of your own.

I quite like Evans, even if the name appears by the thousands in Wales. It means son of Evan, a little sexist by today's standards, but to date no one has decreed the name should be abolished. I admit that along side Griefenhagen and Bazelowski or Almighty Voice and Crazy Horse, Evans could stand a little colour. As for Ronald, that's what my mother called me, the emphasis on each syllable changing, depending on what I had done and the mood she was in. A staccato burst with a hard r meant I was in trouble. On the other hand, drawn out in a plaintive tone, preceded by an "Oh no" and I could feel the guilt descending. But most of the time it was a sound that carried with it warmth and affection. Gradually, Ron took over at school and elsewhere. I liked that, less formal, a sign that one had somehow arrived, although between them the *r* and the *n* never seemed to come out quite solid enough, like there should be something more to follow. In Costa Rica, we discovered that Ron in Spanish means rum; that has a bit more finish to it.

Some people take years to come into possession of their name. I have a friend, a Roman Catholic sister who received all her early training prior to the changes which occurred in her church. She has a picture of herself from those early years dressed in her habit, a beautiful white garment, only the oval of her face in sight. Somewhere beneath the folds is the woman I have come to know as Margaret. The most interesting part of the story, however, is not the clothes she was required to wear, but the name given her by the church. At a certain point it was decreed that she would no longer be Margaret but Robert, the name of her brother.

Giving a woman the name of her brother is different than the naming which goes on in town. One Eyed Bill says something about the man; he has one eye and he's still Bill. And while George the Jerk may not be that complimentary, it leaves him with at least part of his personality intact. But to give a woman a man's name, under the seal of God's approval no less, is quite another matter. It's even more powerful than to leave a person with no name at all. With no name you can at least rest in the comfort of not existing. But to be given, as an adult, a name opposite to your gender?

I try to imagine it; I am no longer Ronald but Angela. Felicity. Hope. I would have a man's body, with all the rights and privileges thereto pertaining, but a woman's name. Johnny Cash sings about just such a situation in which a father names his son Sue in the belief it would make the boy a fighter and help him face the trials of life. If you can believe the song, the plan worked; the boy must fight at every turn to defend his honour, but concludes that if he has a son of his own he will name him anything but Sue. As for my friend Margaret, I am glad to say she not only remains a sister in good standing in her order, but has reclaimed both her own clothes and her name.

Surely there are folk, however, who have an even rougher road, who must contend not just with the difficulty of a name given by parents or church, but rather must live with the confusion imposed by creation. God, or whoever was responsible, either by design or neglect, or perhaps as part of a great joke, brings forth a woman who discovers she has the sex of a man or a man who knows he should have been a woman. I have no idea what it must be like for those who, finding the confusion too much to endure, take drastic measures and obtain a sex change via surgery. Or take no action and endure the confusion.

If I didn't have the name I do I would choose Yitzhak, Hebrew for Isaac. It was the name given by Abraham and Sarah to their son, born when both of them were "stricken with old age." Sarah was over eighty, "after the manner of women" at any rate. We marvel at that, and at Abraham who was a hundred. But it's the name they gave their son that interests me: Yitzhak. Not a weak, limp name meant to whisper weakly off the tip of your tongue through wizened lips, but rather a word heaved from the belly, striking the top of your throat and thrown from your mouth. Proud. Defiant. And for good reason.

In translation Isaac means "to be capable of laughter." He was given this name because Sarah laughed when she was told she would have a child, a laughter you can understand. The story goes that Abraham, at the command of God, took Isaac up onto a mountain to be sacrificed when he was twelve. As the knife is raised, God stops Abraham, and a ram is offered up instead. In part this story is about child sacrifice and how it was no longer to be practiced. Elie Wiesel, holocaust survivor, takes the story one step further. He suggests that Isaac was the first to survive annihilation, the first survivor of the holocaust. Isaac is a name that is both a belly laugh and a soul's lament.

In the course of a life time we acquire many names. In 1972 I was working in a psychiatric hospital in California when an older woman was admitted, diagnosed as manic depressive or bi-polar. Whatever the terminology, when this woman was up she was way up, and when she was down she was very down. On the afternoon I first met her she was in the midst of a manic phase sitting in the admission area awaiting the attention of the nursing staff. She saw me and at once inquired what I did around the place. I began with some answer or other when she cut in and said, "Oh, a competent chaplain son-of-a-bitch." How that fevered brain came up with that unlikely combination of words I have no idea, but as is so often the case with mental illness, a certain wisdom emerged. In her troubled state she had managed to articulate what I believe each of us desires: to be known — not just as kind, honest, and loving — but for all that we are, an insight which it often takes the mad to appreciate.

At any rate, I shall not forget the title bestowed upon me by one troubled and broken woman. Like the title preacher, competent-chaplain-son-of-bitch remains one of my names; I cannot disown it anymore than Albert could escape the title Windy.


To be named by your mother and father is a custom, a necessity. To be named by your community, who knows your sins and your virtues, becomes a blessing.

# I took some comfort there

I'm driving the garbage truck to help my neighbour Gerry who works for the town and picks up garbage every Monday morning. There are usually about twenty stops, depending on how many people have spent the weekend at their cottage. To make a good fellow of myself I said I would help, the reason easy to admit to, the one I hope will be noticed.

Partly it's the truck; I always wanted to drive a truck like this one. I have my own, red and sleek with a racing stripe, air conditioned, the kind of vehicle that when you clean and polish it up and pull in at the lumberyard the young guy behind the counter says, "Nice lookin' truck. What year's that?" They don't say that about the town truck. It's beige with a red door, the one Gerry replaced last year after he hit a tree. Only one window works, the handle's missing on the other. The brake light stays on all the time. Between the roar of the motor and the rattles you know it's the town truck coming long before you ever see it.

No one would admit it, but I think there is a bit of competition involved as to who will drive. Charlie, a mechanic and construction worker all his life, now retired, drives whenever the opportunity arises. So does Art. But Gerry says Art drives too fast, making him run to keep up between stops. And although driving the old town truck would not seem to be a woman's first choice of work, even Gerry's wife Joan appears to find satisfaction in wheeling the old machine around town. To be asked to drive then, having lived in the town for only two years, I felt as if I had arrived, a moment I could not pass up, even if it did disrupt my morning.

In an effort to discipline myself I have a schedule, of sorts, that says I am to sit at my desk and write every morning. This I find difficult. Writing, as everyone knows who has tried it, tends to be a lonely business that requires spending long periods of time playing with words, going wherever they lead, and fearing that much of the time they are headed in the wrong direction. There is always the temptation to get up and run away to some activity — exercise, shopping, visiting — anything where the requirements are clear and the outcome assured. I tell myself I should be more disciplined, but when Gerry asked if I'd drive, writing didn't stand a chance

"Turn at the next alley. Two houses in. They were here last week."

We skid to a stop in front of a pile of black bags. I slip the old truck into park and wait while Gerry hops out and begins loading.

Black garbage bags. My mind turns back thirty years to California and working with a group of patients in a mental hospital. Each of the patients had been given a magazine from which they were to select a picture. The group would then choose one picture to role play. It was a way in which we hoped to lure depressed, sofa bound souls into a bit of motion, interrupt their loneliness and develop a little self-confidence. I have no idea what it did for the patients, but those of us in charge were quite proud of our efforts.

I still remember a particular morning and the woman whose picture was chosen-a young mother of about thirty-five named Kathleen who had been in and out of treatment for over three years. She was getting better, and it was thought she was near discharge. The picture she chose, an advertisement for Glad garbage bags, consisted of a large house with a beautiful lawn on which sat a row of five neatly tied black bags. It was this scene we enacted.

Three people were chosen to play the house, two knelt as a bench. Others stood waving in the wind as trees. Five individuals, neatly seated on the floor became the garbage bags, bulging and waiting to be opened. We all waited in high anticipation for Kathleen to get into her

garbage. Were we not in a mental hospital and were we not in the business of cleaning up our "garbage"? Everyone has garbage; good therapy
dictates that you work on it. We waited and encouraged, but to no
avail; Kathleen adamantly refused to discuss anything in the scene,
especially the five bags. Instead, she sat watching, a slight smile crossing her face, her head nodding in recognition.

Finally she spoke. "Look, it's taken me three years to get all my shit
gathered together and I'm not going to touch it." Kathleen went home
at the end of the week.


"Cats. You wouldn't believe the smell that can build up in those cans."
Gerry waves me forward. "They put the cat shit in a single plastic bag
and the bag breaks. I just throw it all in the truck loose. What a mess.
Turn at the corner."

As we drive along it occurs to me that I am doing something I could
never have done, even imagined doing, if I had stayed in the city. To be
a garbage man in Saskatoon you need blue coveralls, a hard hat, and
leather boots with steel toes. The job requires three men, one driving and
two hopping on and off to dump the cans. People watch from their windows, but never speak. Or there are vinyl bins in the back alleys standing
like tombstones every fifty yards, big enough to hold garbage from four
houses for a week. Great white machines, Department of Public Works,
City of Saskatoon printed on the side, appear any time of day or night
with a beeper warning everyone to stay clear. Sitting way up in front,
looking like a pilot on a 727, sits one man pushing buttons. Makes Gerry
and I with the old truck look like a horse and buggy on the freeway.

We meet Hazel, out for the morning paper, and stop to talk. She
tells us about the wind that blew her tomatoes over in the night. I turn
down the alley where Charlie waves and shouts, "Who the hell you got
drivin' today?" I like Charlie, rough around the edges, but a good soul.
It occurs to me that for all my pleasure in being alone I need these people, need to drive the truck and pick up garbage. A little comfort in my
loneliness. When you say it that way it doesn't sound so bad.

Back in second year university, my grades poor and wondering why
I was there in the first place, I came upon an old sermon written by

Paul Tillich entitled "Alone, Loneliness and in Solitude." He made the point that for all the people around us, we are, at critical moments in our lives, alone. Birth and death, being fired or divorced, these are passages that no one can accomplish for us or even with us. Moreover, such times are accompanied by loneliness. More people, more entertainment, more activity, working harder, only sharpens the feeling.

But loneliness may also be a beginning, says Tillich, an opening into what he called solitude. Solitude can break out at any moment — listening to music, remembering another person, walking alone on the prairie. I like to go to a large city like Toronto or New York and set out walking with my address printed on my hand and enough money set aside to pay for a taxi home if I get lost. There are strange sights and a different language around every corner. Something different for lunch. I don't know a soul and no one knows where I am. Then, without warning, it can happen. You can't make it happen, but sometimes it breaks out, that feeling of peace and belonging, the conviction that life is a friendly place with a human shape.

To be human is to be alone and lonely; solitude is to be alone with one's God.

"Nothing here ... he lives alone. She's gone, an amicable settlement so I hear. He likes his space and so does she. Gave her ten thousand and everyone's happy. One last stop at that brown shed and we're done."

In less than an hour we have gathered all the garbage and head for the dump. We are greeted by the attendant, a friendly character who operates the dump for a living. Like dogs who take on the looks of their owners, this man and the dump have things in common. The one button remaining on his shirt threatens to break and scatter whatever is piled behind it. His beard looks like there might be things hidden in it. But his eyes and little half-smile are friendly and welcoming.

"Where 'bouts you want this?"

"Just over there on the west end. Back in and get everything into the hole. If you back too far we got a tractor here this morning and can pull you out. Or, if you want, we can push you in all the way. We offer service. No job should be left half done."

We dump the garbage and head for home. Without a load I get the truck up to almost eighty. "Not too fast," Gerry says. With the windows down the wind blowing in our faces, we leave a plume of dust on the gravel road. I feel strangely satisfied with my wasted morning.

# at prayer

I'm wearing my clogs today, the third day of April. Ordinarily neither the day nor my footwear are all that outstanding, but together they bring a distinctive kind of pleasure: like going for lunch with an old friend. Or, after a long struggle to find the right words, being surprised by a line that says just what you want.

The shoes aren't much. They're patterned off the Dutch kind once carved from wood. Mine are plastic, subdued brown, but they look like the originals: boat-like creations open at the back so you can slip in and out without missing a step. I drilled holes in the toe of one to see if it helped with ventilation; it did, but the holes let in water as easily as they did air. The damage has since been repaired with a caulking gun and some glue.

When I first bought the shoes over four years ago I thought they were just for garden work, a step above going in your bare feet. Before long, however, I found myself wearing them to visit the neighbours, even going into the city. I don't wear them to the theatre but you could. How satisfying it is to step into clogs at the back door and walk out without first having to sit down, pull on boots, lace them up, and clomp off like a dray horse pulling a load. Coming back I like even better. No boots to remove in order to cross the living room floor. Or, as usually happens, I think I can make it, boots and all, and no one will notice. But no matter how careful I am, Norma invariably observes: "Someone left dirt on the floor." And there's the evidence: a bit of mud or a clump of snow about to become a pool of dirty water. Not so with clogs: just step out of them and keep on going without leaving behind so much as a boot print or the coolness that can linger after an exchange of words.

It's safe now for clogs. The snow has retreated, given up the fight save for a stubborn rear guard action waged in the trees and along the north side of the park. Total surrender will come by the weekend. In the backyard it's dry enough to go for a walk.

Everything remains just as we left it last October; the ground raked, tools in the shed, the lilac bush waiting to be moved. The pergola I built needs a bit of finishing. Winter had obscured it all, but here it is, friendly, waiting. Yet something is different. Our chatter obscures what we cannot describe. Dried grass, a sparrow that didn't make it, the faint smell of rotting leaves. A kind of pleasure seeps in, a pleasurable sadness you could say, the dead everywhere. You can't name it, don't want to, the same reluctance that comes in church when you are all alone. Or on a street corner in New York. An absence of some sort that can frighten.

Maybe that's why here in Saskatchewan we find spring a risky business, and understand why April is the cruellest month of all. At its best it won't last long. And yet ...

You look about and see everyone, everything, more than willing to take the chance. A robin back early, with no worms to eat, huddled in a tree. Gophers on the hill, most of whom haven't a hope of surviving more than a month or two, just long enough, if they're lucky, to get off a litter. A cruelty in it all, but no one's leaving. It's as if a promise has been accepted. A mood of prayer prevails.


I have been reading a book on kaddish, the most beautiful of prayers, uttered across centuries by Jews. Let me say that while I have read a considerable amount about Judaism, the more I learn the more the mystery deepens. I tell myself to go carefully; this tradition belongs to someone else and maybe I shouldn't be here at all.

In the view of the rabbis, anytime there are ten men gathered for the fulfillment of an obligation of prayer or an obligation of study they must sanctify, hallow the occasion, by saying kaddish. Kaddish punctuates a particular occasion with a blessing. Most often, however, kaddish has been associated with death and mourning. A son is called upon to say kaddish for his dead father, the Mourner's Kaddish.

I asked my rabbi friend about kaddish. He informed me that indeed you need ten men to say it, ten present to activate it, so to speak. This requirement has been modified so that women can now make up the number or quorum. At first glance, the rule of ten seems an odd requirement, a technicality which flies in the face of all the assumptions that are made about God and easy accessibility. Can't we just dial up Jesus any time?

The need for ten in order to say kaddish serves as a reminder that you need people to pray; prayer is a community matter. Some rabbis have said the community is so important that a person's prayers are heard by God only when offered as part of a congregation. All of which might remind Christians that prayer need not, must not, become too solitary a business. Too many distortions creep in. Too easy to end up talking to oneself. God is harder to manipulate with ten.

More interesting still, kaddish, for centuries a prayer offered for the dead in synagogues and in concentration camps alike, never mentions grief. It says nothing about the dead and certainly nothing about the mourner. No mention of my feelings. No sign of unconditional positive regard. Rather than an insult, however, this focus away from the self can come as something of a relief.

Kaddish is not always said because the person feels like doing it. Often it is said for reasons of duty or obligation. Or it can be said when one feels gratitude. In short, the saying of kaddish does not depend on the particular state of my being — whether I feel good or not, whether I want to pray or not.

Kaddish remains a hymn of praise, a celebration in remembrance of "He who makes peace in His high places." It is a blessing upon God, that God's name may be lifted up, "magnified and sanctified" in the world God has created, the time of death no exception.

Would it be sacrilege to say kaddish for my purposes, to say kaddish now that winter's gone and spring has come? I feel a deep gratitude for life. And a certain fear. An apprehension. I made it. No, we made it.

The gophers. The robins. The buds on our grandson's oak tree. We made it one more time. It would not be good to die in winter; the ground is so hard and there are so few flowers. It would be better to die in the spring or the fall. Whatever the time, today I can say we made it. A pleasure tempered by the signs.

Would it be permissible to borrow kaddish? To say kaddish when I don't know how. Would it be permitted to say kaddish here in the garden in our clogs —brown and blue, green and canary yellow plastic clogs?

But where are the ten. Counting the women there are still only four of us. Make do. A gopher and three robins comes to eight. There's nothing else to be done — count the magpie and the grackle.

I slip into my office, return with a prayer book and in our clogs we say Kaddish, words of blessing on the One who created all things, who has given and who will take away.

> Magnified and sanctified
> may His great name be praised
> in the world that He created
> as He wills,
> and may His kingdom come
> in your lives and in your days
> and in the lives of all the house of Israel,
> swiftly and soon,
> and say Amen!
>
> Amen
> May His great Name be blessed
> Always and forever!
>
> Blessed
> and Praised
> and Glorified
> and Raised
> and Exalted
> and Honoured
> and Uplifted

and Lauded
Be the Name of the Holy One
(He is blessed!)
Above all blessings
and hymns and praises and consolations
that are uttered in the world,
and say all Amen!

May a great peace from heaven —
and life! —
be upon us and upon all Israel,
and say all Amen!

May He who makes peace in His high places
make peace upon us and upon all Israel,
and say all Amen!

(Kaddish is over 2000 years old, appearing originally in Aramaic. It can be viewed as one of the efforts of the early rabbis to teach their people that in all things, even in death and grief, we are called upon to give thanks to the One who has given life).

# breakfast at Peter D's

"Coffee?"

"Yes."

Bernice leans across the table in front of me, the collar of her white blouse inches away, a hint of perfume in the air. At five-feet-six with a Barbara Streisand nose, dressed in a leather skirt, nylons, and black shoes, and hair kept on the wild side, Bernice has her own beauty.

"Do you want to order or wait for the others?" She steps back. Her dark brown eyes could scorn you or love you.

"I could be the only one this morning. I'll have some brown toast and jam and wait awhile."

"Sure. You can order more later." She pauses a moment. "Say, what happened to Allan? I haven't seen him in weeks?"

"He moved to Ontario ... been gone for three months now."

"He was ... different ... had a real sense of humour. I liked that."

The minutes pass and it becomes obvious that I will be alone for breakfast. Our group has dwindled of late. Obviously coming to breakfast at 7:30 on a Thursday morning in mid-summer is not a high priority on anyone's list. But I like coming. I would like to say I come because I'm interested in what everyone is doing; that is hardly the truth. Clergy talking shop can be tedious, but I have learned to be careful in my criticism. Even on the dullest morning, the breakfast special and an hour's conversation, whatever its nature, provide a little sustenance. Meagre rations some days, but enough to keep the body intact and the spirit alive, hoping against hope for more. And more can happen, I remind myself, right here on a Thursday morning in this booth at Peter D's with the pink walls, flowered carpets, and the philodendrons hanging from the ceiling, it can happen.

I sit there suddenly caught up in a scene from six weeks before. Harold and Carl are sitting by the window. I can't remember who else. The hubbub of the restaurant falls away, leaving us alone as if we were in a cocoon. The room takes on a softer light. Even the quiet ones are speaking. Words take on a life of their own, rushing back and forth, filling the space between us, accomplishing far more than we had intended. Carl tells us something that happened when he was in Lethbridge. Harold explores the depths of a theological mystery. No one is listening. But there is no need to. For a moment we are in Jerusalem: Parthians, Medes, Elamites, and residents of Mesopotamia, Judea, and Cappadocia, all speaking, and we are all understood. For a moment our isolation has been broken. We can hear and know that we have been heard. And we have had nothing stronger than the coffee at Peter D's.

A group of my friends enjoying breakfast at Peter D's
served by our favourite waitress, Bernice.

"There you go." Bernice sets the plate of buttered toast before me. She swings the coffee pot over the table with an abandon perfected through the years, amber liquid streaming through the air, piling up in my cup, stopping with a quarter inch to spare. "I'll be back in a bit when you decide what you want."

She moves away among the tables, filling cups and taking orders. How young she looks.

"O that I were young again …" I hear the words and then I see them. In a book, on the right hand page, half-way down.

It's the only line of the poem I can quote. But I know the piece and I know what was going on. Yeats was sitting on a park bench or maybe at a sidewalk café. A young woman passes on the street. How, he asks, can he ever concentrate on politics, be concerned with wars, or any of life's great issues when, in fact, he has but one desire: "O that I were young again…"

I was wrong; I can remember two lines. How depressing if I should forget the second. Without it the first is but a complaint. But I remember both lines, side by side. And the space between them. "O that I were young again / and held her in my arms." A young man's suffering and an old man's remembering.

"Bernice, do you have a piece of paper?"

"Sure." She disappears through the swinging doors into the kitchen.

I sit watching the cars passing on the street below. Suddenly at the end of my table appears another figure, Deloris, a well-meaning Roman Catholic sister who I have known for a number of years. She has a strong need to be friendly and at once the chatter begins.

"That story you told on Sunday … the one about the young Jewish man who was Hasidic who loves a woman and wants to marry her. But her parents are Orthodox and forbid it. They finally marry, but he dies … I forget the ending and I want to use it in a presentation on prayer I'm giving next week." Deloris trails on at length, pleading with me to go over the ending one more time.

She doesn't realize it, but she's meddling with my favourite Hasidic tale. There is something so fragile about the story, so painful and so beautiful, I want to protect it. I want to shout at her to go away, she can't have the story because she'll mess with it and screw it all up. But she must get everything just right. A script for all occasions. It's the same when she plays the piano; every note must be perfect, like she's hanging on to the little buggers for fear they will get loose and enjoy themselves.

"You can't memorize a story like that, Deloris. It's like making love; you just have to do it. Enjoy it ... mistakes can help ..."

"You can't be perfect, you mean. That's good. I'll have to mark that down." She fumbles in her immense handbag and finds a pen. "But could you just refresh my memory ... especially the last lines?" I give in and tell her the story.

"How does that last line go again?"

"When the messiah comes he will put his arm around the young man and say 'But what is that to you and me, for I have come for all those who are not right'."

"Thanks. " She flutters away and I return to watching the cars on Eighth street.


"Here's a pad. All I can find. Will this do?" Bernice seems pleased with what she has found.

"Sure ... that's perfect."

I settle in to write, intent on capturing the events of the morning on paper. But after twenty minutes I have next to nothing on the page; whatever it was I intended has escaped my scribbles. I crumple the paper and stuff it in the cup to soak up the remains of my coffee.


"Do you want something more?" Bernice stands back from the table. Her eyes have a warmth to them, a hint of laughter.

"No ... no thank you. The toast will be enough."

"Have a good day then ... see you in two weeks."

# from a distance

Without warning, it's as if the tide has come in, surrounding me and eroding my little bit of sand. My space has been inundated by a ragged band of preschoolers, led by two women, making their way across the campus on a field trip. The lead woman forms a kind of maypole from which extends invisible streamers, each attached to a small figure. Clearly some of the streamers are stretched to the breaking point, others hang limp.

I have often said I am not fond of little children. W.C. Fields' pronouncement "Anyone who hates children and dogs can't be all bad," has always appealed to me. When people have asked about this I have just laughed and said that children are apt to smell funny and do unexpected things.

I have been able to admire children at a distance, but close up something happens. Baptizing children was difficult. I always admired priests who could take the babies from their mothers and carry them about. I imagined myself doing that, holding the infants up, walking down into the congregation, offering them up to the sky and the people, holding them close, nestled in the folds of my robe, talking to them. But some invisible barrier intervened.

I once read that Franz Kafka had an abhorrence of touching human flesh. Is it that touching a child, the sensation of skin on skin repels me? Yes. But the touch of some skin I have quite enjoyed. Why should I avoid children? What is there about the thought of holding them, looking closely at their fragile features, that requires me to keep a distance?

Working in the hospital it was the children that troubled me. I could be with the adults, come close to them in their pain, sit with a family when there had been a death. But I remember the first time a child died, a little boy, about five, with cancer. The father was there standing by the bed, weeping, talking to his son. The supervisor said I hurt because I had a son and identified with the man. Maybe. But I distrust such neat explanations.

The forward progress of my visitors slows a moment, allowing time for everyone to regroup, the runaways retrieved and the stragglers recovered. One little girl, Oriental, her clothes neat, hair trimmed, with a complexion as smooth and bright as petals on a rose, stops within three feet of my bench, unafraid. She studies me a moment, wide-eyed, innocent, then moves on with the grace and composure of a strolling empress surveying her garden. Other children run, shouting, asking questions.

A second woman enters the park and, just behind her, one lone child, who I suspect will be late most of his life and will look upon all gatherings of people at a distance. He has the walk of an old man, more a hobble than a step. He looks ahead, as if scanning the horizon for some sign of the end or for reinforcements. I fancy I hear him saying "slow down," or perhaps "Why the hell are we doing this anyway?" I am sure that field trips are not his first love. A part of me wants to call out to the woman that some people don't like field trips. Leave the boy on the bench with me, pick him up on the way back.

After a brief rest, the group begins its uneven progress, one lone figure bringing up the rear.

# let your light so shine

"Mr. Evans?"

"Yes."

A rather plain looking woman of perhaps thirty-five stood before me nodding to herself, scanning the green and yellow pages of my file. After a moment she looked up, the suggestion of a smile on her face, a hint of mischief in her eyes.

"Come with me, Ronald," she said.

Far from a command, I felt I had received an invitation. The words rolled off her tongue, warm and friendly, equal emphasis on both *come* and *me*, followed by a little pause, the kind of space that people speak of in which they say their whole life flashes before them. In this case, I had images of an old movie where the leading lady, all eyes and bosom, makes an offer the hero can't resist.

I have heard similar voices and encountered the same looks on dance floors. And from a waitress in town at my favourite restaurant who understands that her voice and looks are as important as the food she serves. But that's life at a dance hall and a restaurant. I didn't expect such a welcome here, not from a clerk admitting me for prostate surgery.

Her body half-turned, beckoning, I followed.

I lay claim, as most men can, to some awareness on the subject of care in the hands of women. The hospitalization of which I speak marks the tenth time over the past sixty years when I have agreed to have my body cut upon, to have pieces removed and broken parts repaired. Nothing life threatening. Tonsils when I was five. Appendix at thirteen. Three bouts at the dentists having most of my teeth extracted. A variety of other relatively minor surgeries, although, when it's your body, nothing seems minor. In this process you see very little of the surgeons. Masks and gowns. Voices, a needle, and the surgeon fades as quickly as the operating room lights. But the nurses are there before and after. When you are most vulnerable, hurt, afraid, it is a woman's voice you hear and hands you feel. It's a woman you want to hear and feel. Close up. Hands on.

I remember the nurse, an older woman, who stabbed my finger for a blood sample when I was five. My mother was holding me in her lap. We were in a dark room with a linoleum floor and everything smelled strange. I can see the little bubble of blood on the end of my finger and the nurse saying "This will be over in a minute." When I was thirteen, a nurse left me alone in a room with a gown and a bottle, saying to get undressed and leave a "sample." She wasn't all that much older than I, a student possibly, and I think was a little embarrassed to tell a young man to pee in a bottle. I didn't know what sample meant and didn't leave one. After that operation another nurse gave me something for pain at night, straightened my bed, and later said I could have ice cream. She wore pale red lipstick, a little perfume, and looked perfect in her white uniform and cap with a white enamel name tag that read Miss Gray. Fifty years later, it was a nurse who finally got a catheter to work after too many hours of waiting. I forget what she looked like except that she will be forever beautiful. And someone is sure to point out that my sister is a nurse. Not only that, I married into the profession.

But, of course, beyond hospitals, there's another realm over which women have reigned supreme — the school room. As a child I heard of one school several miles away that had a man for a teacher. It was not until I was in Grade 11 that I experienced a man behind the teacher's desk.

Over the years, while a few of the teachers were boring and one or two were terrorists, most of them were at least average. Some were excellent. Of this latter group, whatever may have been their qualifications, it is not professional expertise for which I remember them. Besides the obvious reason — that they treated me with respect — I can now recognize, dare admit, that I liked certain of them because they were women — who were not my mother.

This is not to criticize my mother nor to deny that there exists some invisible, mysterious tie between mothers and sons. I have read that soldiers wounded in the midst of battle call out for their mothers. And when we marry, that other field of battle, the theory is we cast about until we find someone like our mother. Or in rebellion choose someone we perceive as a total opposite, only to find that nothing has changed and a bond becomes an apron string.

There is a part of a boy's education, a learning that does not cease, that is best left to women other than his mother.

I remember Miss M. who came to our school when I was in Grade 4, following the bitter days of a chalk-throwing battle-axe. Miss M. read a chapter of a book after lunch, a practice which may account in part for my continuing love of reading. She would sit at the front of the room with her legs resting on a stool in such a way that all the little boys could see up her skirt. We always thought Leonard had it best because he sat in the front row. I thrived under Miss T., a woman who had been in the Canadian Air Force in the war and liked her beer. She was the first teacher to call me Ron. But it was Miss S. I remember most fondly, delightfully feminine and a bit plump in all the right places. She came for only part of a year after the regular teacher fell ill, a misfortune for which I have always been grateful. I remember Miss S. leaning over my desk to help with a problem; her perfume and her cotton dress, not to mention her breasts only inches away, had all the boys giggling. I didn't know exactly what was going on, but whatever it was it seemed like a good thing.

I am sure the woman at the admission desk didn't plan what she was doing, didn't consciously swivel her hips and say to herself, "Turn it on. Give this old guy a thrill." Or maybe she did and, if so, God bless her. Perhaps she had heard the command that her sexuality was neither to be hidden under a bushel nor thrown down in the street.

In a day when there's much conflict, so much that is proper and not proper, so much lost, it's difficult to know how to write about one's relationship with women. One does not lack for advice. Develop your identity as a man. Male bonding may help. Your feminine side needs attention. Such language makes me nervous; the intent may be right, but after awhile I want to go and take a shower. Only rarely can one find a voice who puts in a good word for lust.

I enjoy my association with men, eating together, a good story told. A kind of understanding sets in of how things are. Often I remember my father and wish he were here to talk with. I know what he liked to eat and I would prepare it for him. There are some stories I want to hear again, some questions that need asking. I like working with my son now, watching him do what he has learned with an efficiency I never had. It is sobering to admit that he is the one who knows, the one familiar with a different world.

Having said all that, I cherish the company of women. And here I am at sixty-five working out the details with little more adequacy than I possessed when I was eighteen, maybe less. A whole new landscape. But there is one thing I now possess that I did not always have in times past: a certain sense of gratitude.

I am grateful for what I received in a hospital hours before surgery, grateful for the grace and style of a woman who gave freely, grateful that I could still hear and accept what was offered. A reminder that even though age changes some things, and everything sooner or later, for now there remains a fragile and indescribable bond with women, brief moments that continue to appear in the most unlikely places.

# in gratitude

This past week was marked by two special events, the first of which was a birthday party. There is a reason why this birthday party was of such significance: it is not just one birthday party but two. Both our kids were born on January 20th, four years apart. We hadn't planned it this way, although with my wife's attention to detail some people think we did.

To celebrate this year, the family went to lunch, a more private get together preceding a larger party later in the week. Our family has increased over the years our son is married and we thought it best to invite his wife to join us. She is expecting, so in a way that meant six at the table. By good fortune we had a small section of the café to ourselves. A part of me sat on the ledge among the naked Greek statues watching in wonder the scene before me.

At the far end of the table sat my wife, in good health, enjoying her family. She and I have had no disagreements — this week at any rate. Our two children, now adults, talk easily with one another. For a moment Julian's promise is being fulfilled: all will be well, all will be well, indeed all manner of things will be well. It has not always been so and may not be in a day or an hour. But it's true now. A sense of well-being that only a table, food, and family can give. Perhaps we could put a little in a doggy bag for to-morrow.

The other major event of the week was Super Bowl Sunday. I must admit I enjoy watching a good football game. There is something about it I find appealing. In the midst of the mayhem and savagery, one detects the presence of a finely tuned and fragile order: the line of a ball spiralling in a graceful ark, a slim body perfectly conditioned streaking forward, both arriving at a predetermined point, blending gracefully together, and continuing on in one seamless movement. Then chaos. Man and ball are driven to the turf, reduced to a crumpled heap by a tackle, perfectly timed and delivered. One moment of beauty destroyed by another.

Yes, I like watching football. That's why I was troubled when my wife reminded me this was also Persephone Sunday, our date to attend the matinee production of the local theatre. The play or the Super Bowl? That was the question. Of course, I could not admit to such a thing for fear of what it would look like. An all out crisis was averted when I realized the game didn't begin until 5:30 p.m. and that we could make it home from the theatre in time, maybe even see the kick off.

Now, a week later, the Super Bowl remains little more than a fast fading memory. For a moment I forget what teams were involved. But the play, Mom's The Word, remains fixed in my mind, the characters and their lines more vivid now than they were a week ago. Six women portray the experience of being mothers: the pain of birth, babies spitting up, the sight and smell of loaded diaper pails, the fear they have of hurting their children, the dumb comments of others, husbands who are not around, husbands who want sex too soon and too often. Yet, regardless of all the trials, there remains in the lives of these women a deep sense of joy and wonder.

One woman told of falling in love with another man; she doesn't realize what is happening. Then she tells you the other man is this bit of life, this little boy who is her son. Her husband tells her it is strange to be in the same room watching his wife fall in love with another man. But that's all right, because he is falling in love with the same guy. I don't cry, I don't cry at movies or plays. Not often, anyway, and don't tell anyone if I do. But I had tears in my eyes this time. I have thought about this a lot since the play, even during the football game.

Tears. For what?

For not being there. I never saw my children born. I saw one an hour after in the arms of a nurse. I heard the other minutes after her arrival. But I was on the other side of the wall. I would have run a mile if someone had suggested I be in the room, but I think I could have handled it. I would like to have been there with my wife. Later, I smelled the diaper pail and changed my share. I looked after the kids from time to time, but too soon I was away and missed too many things. I weep for not seeing my children born. Or is it for not seeing them grow up?

I weep too for not understanding, not knowing. I realize that ignorance does not mean one can claim innocence. All I know is that thirty-five years after the fact, I did not know what it was to be a father. Babies, little children, mothers: a scene of chaos where I am slowly beginning to perceive another delicate thread of order at work, a beginning to which I could have contributed more — but didn't.

Do I wish I could do it over again and this time get it right? Yes, but not for long. Trying to get it right is generally a mistake, one that takes up too much time. There is a line from T.S. Eliot concerning his efforts at writing poetry: "So here I am ... trying to learn to use words, and every new attempt / Is a wholly new start, and a different kind of failure... "

Yes, I feel guilt over all the things that might have been. But not for long. Those are memories to keep and visit, but not to live in. The tears are for something far more precious. There are feelings that must not be lost amid all the others, another thread of order that must not go unnoticed, for it transforms everything.

A relative of mine once told me of her father who was an alcoholic, but had gained sobriety through Alcoholics Anonymous. On occasion, he would speak of his recovery, each time beginning to cry when he talked of his family. Each time he was overcome with the reminder that through all his drinking, his family had not abandoned him.

Tears come, then, for a lot of reasons: fear, anger, hurt, and there are those that come in gratitude. Somehow, against all odds, we are here. At the table. For an hour. A day. Eating and drinking and able to say, "Full of wounds, but still standing."

# a time beyond fixing

I can see them, hear them: my father and a few of his friends, men most often, sitting around the kitchen table. There is food and, on the occasions I have in mind, Johnny Walker whiskey. Two fingers to a glass. A voice calls out, "By God, it's good to be here."

"Damn right," comes a reply.

My father raises his glass. Others follow. They pause, look about at each other, laughing. Thrusting his glass in the air Father shouts, "Here's lookin' at ya." Together they tip their heads and throw back the whiskey.

"Here's lookin at ya." I have learned in subsequent years that other people act and speak in different ways on such occasions. Poles shout *"Nazdrovie. Danes roar skol."* Still others, more English, say *"To your health,"* or *"Cheers."* For Jews there are words that carry a note of declaration and commitment: *lachaim*, to life.

The truth is at this late hour I am still learning what it means to celebrate, to recognize the moment.

Celebration back in the hills was looked upon with a certain suspicion: people enjoying themselves, and, too often, enjoying themselves too much. If you celebrated you did so when the work was done, when you had nothing better to do. Life tended to be divided in two: hard work and hard pleasure, that latter confined to Saturday nights and New Year's Eve.

At church we found mention of celebration uncomfortable. Celebration of a funeral? A wedding, perhaps. The Roman Catholics celebrate mass, but what does that mean? Religion was a solemn business whose goal it was to point out our sins and help us overcome them. When we were finished with this, there was a whole world that required our assistance.

In college I discovered psychology, which promised to help me understand my sins, their origin within the neurosis of my family, and, once possessing such insight, I would be free to make better choices. When you are pure enough, the church said, then you may celebrate, albeit carefully. When you are healthy enough, psychology said, you will be free to raise your glass, to shout *a skol* or proclaim *lachaim*. My father and his friends, whatever their excesses, knew better than that.

Celebration. I asked my friends what it meant and they said, "A party, a good time, food." The dictionary said to honour or observe some special occasion, to praise. I asked a friend, a priest by trade, and he at once said celebration suggests "People, memory, a meal." I put the question to my friend Roger, a rabbi. Everyone needs a priest and a rabbi among his friends.

We met over lunch and as always I felt a certain caution, fearful I might crush something. Not that Roger is fragile. Rather this man is one of the toughest souls I know and possesses a formidable intellect, which he brings to every discussion. Yet, he touches a sadness in me. Or maybe I'm just intimidated. Whatever the case, my appreciation for him began some years ago when he lost his wife in a car accident. He told me then that within the Jewish tradition there is a structure, designed to provide comfort in times of grief.

"I know now," he said, "that it works. In the first week after a death one is not required to do anything, not even to pray. You are to be cared for by the community in every way. In my case, all I wanted was for someone to hold me while I wept. And this they did."

Another incident had not been so helpful, although even as Roger told about it he could laugh. Some well-meaning folk in his congregation had concluded that it would be helpful if he met with two other men, one a writer and the other a psychiatrist, both of whom had lost their wives at about the same time. The friends arranged for the three grieving men to go to supper together. In the course of the evening, the psychiatrist announced that he had concluded he was not going to grieve; it might upset his patients.

Most memorable to me, however, was the funeral for Roger's wife. I had only been in a synagogue a few times before and never to a Jewish funeral. Many of us, the men at any rate, sat upright, self-conscious, anxious our yarmulkes would slip from our heads. Yet inwardly, for myself at any rate, a sense of awe prevailed, a feeling of delight at this strange, new world I had entered for an hour.

A visiting rabbi officiated. He began with a welcome and prayers that I was not familiar with. Then he announced, "I now call upon Rabbi Pavey to speak." I will forever remember those words. They had a tone to them, not of an invitation or an order, but rather a ring of command, the kind of thing spoken to troops before battle or athletes who must face invincible opponents; this day it is required of you.

For some fifteen minutes, in one of the most moving speeches I have ever heard, Roger spoke of his wife and his memories of her. I recall one story in particular.

"We were quite young when we first met. I finally worked up the courage to ask her for a date. I took her for fish and chips, and then walked her home. Then I proposed and she accepted. She said afterward that if I had not done it, she would have done it for me. And we never regretted it."

Roger concluded with a question, "Has it all been worth it, you may ask?" He paused an instant, then continued, "I can say yes. And I would do it all over again."

Over our soup and sandwich Roger mentions his arthritis which takes an increasing toll. On this particular day, near the end of October, he had just completed his twenty-sixth service and twenty-sixth sermon of the month. For reasons I don't understand October is an especially involved time within the tradition. He tells me the time is approaching when he must terminate his relationship with his congregation and decide what to do with his life, given his remaining energy.

It was in the midst of all this that I told him I was looking into the matter of celebration and wondered what it meant to him.

"I am reminded," he said, "of a blessing we use upon going to the bathroom. It is a thanksgiving that everything still works, or at least works as well as it does. To celebrate is not something one does on occasion, when you feel good. You do it at all times and in all places; it is a commandment. And I don't mean an order handed down by God, I don't believe in a God who goes around telling people what to do. You celebrate out of a desire to give thanks, in gratitude. Because when all is said and done, life has been given. It is a gift. Life has been given and one celebrates. It is a command that arises out of desire."

"But what of the days when I cannot?" I asked.

"Oh, surely there are those times. It can't be any other way. Celebration can't be ordered up or guaranteed. But that is where the community comes in. They will do what you cannot do, remember what you forget. Some day you will be called upon to do the same for them. "


To celebrate, the rabbi said, is a commandment, one that arises not because of some divine edict or a dictate of one's guilt ridden conscience. Rather, celebration arises out of gratitude, a desire to give thanks for life. The priest said it takes people, memory, a meal.

# a good funeral

"God, I'm glad I am in here and not out there on that damn farm."

Such was my father's assessment of his move to the city and the beginning of retirement. His attitude surprised us for we thought he would never make the adjustment. Most of his close friends had died. His familiar haunts were miles away. Even his little red truck had been left behind. The truth was he was relieved; the farm had become too much for him, and he felt he had become a burden to his neighbours, and an embarrassment to himself. Free of the burden, a new found peace emerged, a sign of which was the bottle of beer that sat in the fridge untouched. Perhaps, it occurred to me, there would be time now when he could enjoy himself and I could enjoy him.

Father had really wanted to be a doctor. All indications are he would have made a good one. Certainly, he made a good amateur veterinarian. I remember helping him deliver a dead calf, the most awful scene I have ever witnessed. He had to remove the calf's exposed head in order to deliver the rest of the body. Blood and shit everywhere. My job was to hold the cow's tail so he could work. With the other hand I held onto the railing for fear I would faint.

To a considerable degree farming was but a necessity, a means of keeping food on the table. His first love was municipal politics, even though it consumed immense amounts of his time. He thrived on the demands placed on him which, I suspect, served as a welcome diversion from family and farming.

In the midst of the great depression the municipal council became the one source of assistance people relied on for survival, a process in which my father as reeve played a pivotal role. I didn't realize it as a child, but I developed an immense pride in him that arose not just from his ability to do things — fill in as the undertaker today and the veterinarian tomorrow — but also from the kind of confidence he displayed in the moment. Calls would come at all hours of the day, sometimes just asking for an opinion on a matter as mundane as the repair of a road, but often because of a death or some other crisis. I came to believe, as I think others did, that everything would be all right because my father was there.

I don't know when I became aware of it, but I could see my father slipping, slowly being destroyed. He was drinking more, often every day, and he was not keeping up to the requirements of the farm. It was not difficult to identify causes: loss of his own father when he was four, a flaw in his personality, alcohol, the demands of a system. The reasons can go on and on, but I have become increasingly skeptical of such an analysis. It seems to be but a futile effort at treatment in absentia, an attempt to figure out what was wrong and dream of what might have been. And not far away lies resentment and ingratitude. Whatever the case now, long after his death, the picture looks much different.

For some reason I had accepted two burdens stemming from my parents. First, I should be angry with them, Father particularly. Anger was in the air, criticism of one's parents a social past time. And who did not have a father who had failed? The books I read and the people I listened to encouraged it. Yet, try as I might, I could find no anger for him. Oh yes, we had argued over different things; I had even told him to go to hell on occasion. But it was a momentary thing. More than anger I felt sadness that he could not find the peace he deserved, and I wish I could have lessened the sense of distance between us. Here I began to recognize the second burden, one more difficult to lay down. As a good child and a dutiful son you were to help your parents, a task which inevitably translated into trying to change them, save them from their own sins, and make them happy. Of course, like trying to keep your spouse happy, this is an unbearable burden and one that was never intended.

I had not planned for it, but one of the benefits of returning to school when I was thirty was a training program, part of which included seeing a psychiatrist for purposes of working on one's personality. It was assumed that if you could smooth out some of your rough edges, you might have a better chance of helping others. A questionable thesis, but neverthe-less I took advantage of the opportunity. I began seeing a woman by the name of Dr. Beach who encouraged me to keep track of my dreams. One afternoon I reported a dream involving my father. He was doing some-thing embarrassing and I "needed to take care of him." The good doctor interrupted, "Did you hear what you said?" We went on to talk about my need to take care of my father, that there was now no reason for that. He was my father, not an invalid. I was a son, not a rehab worker. It began my process of sorting out our relationship and laying down burden.

It took me five years to realize that for all his deficiencies, the argu-ments we had, the times when I wished he were different, there were good times and these I remembered. He was a good father and I loved him. And I knew I must speak with him. He and I had never done such a thing, although I think we always knew by some intuition where the other was at. But now, before it was too late I decided to tell him. Not too directly, I told myself, only as much as he could handle. At least it seemed that he would be the one to experience the difficulty.

My parents had come for a visit. The evening before their departure Father was sitting alone in his room. I knew I must speak now or perhaps never. I sat down on the bed with him and told him there was something I wanted to tell him. "I want you to know you have been a good father to me and I am proud of you." He started to say something about things being hard at times and Mother having a tough time of it. I am sure I was hearing some of his guilt for what had happened in the past. But I stopped him and said that I was talking about him. "I want you to know you have been a good father to me." He nodded and we sat together for a few minutes as close as if we had been digging potatoes or forking hay. His hands were huge beside mine and I could smell his sweat.

Later, Mother was to report she had never seen him so pleased with life as he was in the weeks following their trip, and she didn't know why.

Years later I was sitting with some friends when one of them remarked, "Did my father ever say anything worth remembering — I can't think of anything." I wanted to stop him and say no, no, that can't be so. How can you say that about your father? I said nothing because I know this is the reality for some people. Nevertheless, it troubled me that the man felt this way toward his father.


St. Valentine's Eve 1976. I received a call that Father had been taken to the hospital. Somehow I knew what to expect; he had done nothing by halves and this would be no exception. We stood about in the quiet room until the doctor came in to tell us what we already knew. They had done everything they could, but he had died almost instantly from the heart attack.

We found him as the doctors had left him, his body covered by a green sheet, a metal tube still in his mouth. He looked as I had seen him many times before, lying on his favourite couch after lunch, asleep. It was as if he would wake and say "you get the horses. I'll be along in a bit." Later, we saw the body at the funeral home after the undertaker had done what undertakers do. Among other things they had put a kind of angelic look on his face, and I knew my father wasn't there.

At first I felt a sense of injustice. Why couldn't he have been given a little more time, a few years to rest and enjoy life? I would have taken him for drives out to the hills. Maybe even have got him to go down east to see his old home and visit a last remaining relative.

We had a good funeral. It was only the third time I could remember my father in anything resembling church. The first time had been at his mother's funeral. The other occasion was one of those spontaneous and usually disastrous ventures for which drinking men are famous. He and two of his best friends had been imbibing all Sunday afternoon and, for reasons known only to them, decided they would go to church that evening. My mother was somewhat perplexed, as was my brother, but there was no discouraging the trio. It would be fitting if I could report that something truly bizarre occurred, that they had embarrassed everyone or that they all had been saved. Such was not the case. The three of them sat there, in their white shirts and ties, perfect gentlemen. They even sang well. Nothing more happened than the church smelled like a tavern for the evening.

As the funeral progressed, I felt a peace descend on the place. The preacher read the 121st Psalm: "Unto the hills do I lift up my eyes / from whence does my help come... " He avoided making Father a saint, but instead took us back to the farm and the kitchen table, and told a story or two that he had heard from Mother. He said Father had gathered us again as he had done many times before.

Then it occurred to me that it had taken Father seventy-six years to get his life in order. It was time now for one last celebration.

# dust to dust

In ones and twos neighbours and friends find their way to the kitchen to visit with my parents. I wander about, trying to be sociable, greeting people I have not seen in years.

Without wanting to admit it, I have my own feelings about giving up the farm, feelings I have tried to avoid. It has been easier to focus on my parents, especially Father. He is the one who will have the most difficulty. How can he ever be persuaded to have a sale? Two months before I had listened as the subject was first raised.

"It ain't worth anything. Junk most of it. Who would buy the stuff?" Flinging one hand in the air, he uttered a final curse, "To hell with it!"

These are familiar words; I had heard them before, even welcomed them on days when we had spent hours digging potatoes until our backs ached. Or forked hay all day in dust and sweat. Indeed, it was a kind of declaration of freedom for all occasions: to hell with pigs, to hell with banks, to hell with everything. For a little while his words had made it so; we were free. But faced with a sale, there can be no such relief, only the auctioneer's attempt at reassurance, at once both a lie and the truth.

"No ... no ... gotta have a sale, Alex. It'll sell. Lots of things here people want. Gather it up. Some day in June when seeding's done we'll have a sale. Hell, yes, gotta have a sale."

My parents have lived on the farm for over fifty years, raised three children, and somehow stayed married while fending off a land company and the bank until good years returned. But now, both over seventy, they face an opponent with whom there can be no negotiation. Reluctantly they have given up "the Hamilton quarter," "Dempsey's," and "the pasture," pieces of ground christened as affectionately as family. Now there must be a sale, a ritual as common to the prairie as selling cattle in the fall.

I can see my mother sorting through her possessions, bits of her life, to be put out on tables, pawed over, then sold for a dollar. And Father arranging his aging machinery in the yard, parading it like a whore on the street, embarrassed at what he is doing. Nevertheless, the auctioneer prevails and in late May the yellow posters appear.

AUCTION SALE. Tractor ... Cultivator ... Pump engine ... Pump jack ... Washer ... Dryer ... Stove. The list went on, naming items of ever decreasing value, then ending as did every sale poster: Other goods too numerous to mention. Lunch served.

Down by the barn the auctioneer stands in a hay rack, pointing to one item after another. The cream can we hauled drinking water in brings four dollars. He comes to a pile of old harnesses that haven't seen the back of a horse in thirty years. Two dollars. Two, Two. Who will give me two? A dollar. Finally a man offers fifty cents for the whole lot. Sold. The tangle of straps and buckles is thrown into the back of a pickup and man drives away, pleased with his bargain. By noon I can take no more and slip away, down the lane past the barn and corrals. I remember the day I saw the last sling full of hay disappear into the loft. "That's the last damn time I'll ever have to do that," I said.

The thought crosses my mind that if I had the money I could keep the farm.

We could come here, plant a garden, maybe even put up a bit of hay. On a rainy evening there would be a kitchen with a wood stove and table. The neighbours would come and drink tea, and talk the language of the land like sailors talk of the sea. The dark times, the hail storms, and the dead milk cow, the fights, and the loneliness, would be forgotten.

I wander on to the well where I find a place to sit in the shade. Often I have come here with a team of horses, a stone boat and two barrels to haul water. It was the best job one could have on a hot day. Just start the engine, an old two cylinder banger, then doze off to the rhythm of the pump jack delivering cold water from the depths. According to my father, the well had been found by a "witcher" who had wandered about for days with a willow rod before giving the order to dig at this particular spot. His assurance that there would be water fifteen feet down was met with skepticism, but at fourteen feet the shovels struck sand, and then water filled to a depth of five feet.

"Best damn well in the country, never went dry," my father would say, and then pause before adding words that haunt every story he tells, "even in the thirties."

In the distance I can hear the auctioneer's voice, pleading for another dollar. Ten feet away a gopher eyes me from behind a mound of earth. Once she would have been no more than a pest to be shot or drowned with a pail of water, but on this day I welcome her, grateful for her presence. Suddenly, she stands upright like a stick, eyeing me, then drops, flicks her tail, and scoots through the grass where she stands again to watch. Trim and saucy, she reminds me of my favourite teacher in Grade 6, a young woman with whom all the boys had fallen in love.

Then, as sudden as a dust devil in the field, the feeling comes, a longing, a desire without a name. I have known it before in the midst of listening to certain music or when walking alone on the prairie. Or when I have drawn close to a woman and thought I could somehow hold the feeling, grasp it, only to have the moment dissolve in pain and disillusionment. Today there is only the gopher, sun, and voices in the distance. Minutes pass. The shadow of a hawk glides across the hillside. The gopher slips from sight. As suddenly as the feeling has come, it passes and I am left alone.


I find my way back to the yard and stand close to Father, one arm on his shoulder, watching as the auctioneer moves to the tractor, "the old Case" as it has come to be known. Father bought it in 1946 for $5,000, a sum which, after the poverty of the thirties, seemed like a fortune. It became his great pride, the first modern tractor in the community, one

My father's LA Case tractor in 1945, which he bought for $5000.
Sporting rubber tires, headlights and a road gear that went 12 miles an hour.
It was his pride and joy.

with rubber tires, lights and even a road gear that went twelve miles an hour. He had fussed over it as if it were a child.

"Five hundred. Who will give me $500? Five. Five. Who'll give me four-fifty?" After a few minutes of haggling the tractor sells.

As we turn away and head back to the house, I finally admit to myself what I have been avoiding all day: I cannot come to this place again. But neither can I abandon it. I will remember the kitchen, the barn. I will remember the well and the gopher. And when I drive along a highway past a weathered, one-eyed barn, past a few maples, and a dying poplar in the corner of a field, I will remember a warm day in June when people gathered and an auctioneer yipped a song of mourning.

# at the gas station

I will always remember
the gas station on the corner
of avenue P and twenty-second

I stopped for gas
the morning my mother died
a strange place for meditation
a crow sounding the mantra
gas fumes for incense

death has been
a discontented passage
but now it is over
the last parent gone
I am no one's child
standing at the edge
of unexplored territory

where to the young
I will be some old guy
and to my children
who countless times have owned
and disowned me
I will be
    father

point man in the platoon
alone
marked for death
first person in the godhead
contaminated with expectations
abba
daddy
father
an unexpected inheritance
I have not always wanted

out here in front
I can see for miles
a long line extending
to the past
a mixed bag of souls
a preacher
one hard drinking miner
a farmer and strong women
for whom exuberance
was not a virtue

check the oil
it's fine and I drive
out onto twenty-second
afraid to admit a subdued
ecstasy
aware
I am the first one
and can see
across the city to prairie
    flat
endless
stretching
    into luminous white

# acknowledgements

I am grateful to the readers of *The Sourdough Bagel,* the "newsletter" I started as a means of learning how to write. Likewise I owe a debt to the Wednesday and Thursday morning breakfast groups whose members provided both encouragement as well as grist for the mill.

My thanks to Dundurn Press, particularly Tony Hawke, who not only offered advice at a crucial moment but suggested that "Saskatchewan" be in the title.

A special thanks to Joyce and Janet for their encouragement and Raymond for his friendship. Among other things they believed there was something worthwhile when I had my doubts. My deepest thanks to Norma, who not only believed, but read everything many times — the best proof reader one could wish for.